D1333416

VGM Opportunities Series

OPPORTUNITIES IN
PRINTING CAREERS

Irvin J. Borowsky

Revised by
Lewis R. Baratz

Foreword by
I. Gregg Van Wert
President
National Association of Printers and Lithographers

VGM Career Horizons
NTC/Contemporary Publishing Company

Library of Congress Cataloging-in-Publication Data

Borowsky, Irvin J.
    Opportunities in printing careers / Irvin J. Borowsky ; revised by
Lewis Baratz ; foreword by I. Gregg Van Wert.
        p.   cm. — (VGM opportunities series)
    ISBN 0-8442-2306-9. — ISBN 0-8442-2307-7 (pbk.)
    1. Printing—Vocational Guidance—United States.   I. Baratz,
Lewis. II. Title. III. Series
Z243.U5B67   1998
686.2'023'73—dc21   97-44574
                                                                                        CIP

Cover photo credits:
Courtesy Vicks Lithograph & Printing Corporation, Yorkville, New York.

Published by VGM Career Horizons
An imprint of NTC/Contemporary Publishing Company
4255 West Touhy Avenue, Lincolnwood (Chicago), Illinois 60646-1975 U.S.A.
Copyright © 1998 by NTC/Contemporary Publishing Company
All rights reserved. No part of this book may be reproduced, stored in a retrieval
system, or transmitted in any form or by any means, electronic, mechanical,
photocopying, recording, or otherwise, without the prior permission of NTC/
Contemporary Publishing Company.
Printed in the United States of America
International Standard Book Number: 0-8442-2306-9 (cloth)
                                                            0-8442-2307-7 (paper)

15   14   13   12   11   10   9   8   7   6   5   4   3   2   1

CONTENTS

ABOUT
THE AUTHOR

Irvin J. Borowsky is the founder and chair of North American Publishing Company, the nation's largest publisher of magazines for the printing and allied graphic arts industries. From his company's inception in 1958, Borowsky's chief objective has been the dissemination of creative ideas for expanding printing company efficiency and profitability.

His commitment to the industry is reflected in the editorial stance of his printing publications, which supply printing and graphic arts executives with the information required to keep them technologically competitive and managerially astute. As a result, Borowsky's printing publications have earned an intensely loyal readership whose numbers have increased in each of the last 32 years. One prime indicator of the firm's success is that it employs more editors, writers, and designers—and sells more advertising —than any other firm serving this field.

Borowsky, author of *Artists United Against Prejudice* and the *Guide to Two-Color Halftone Printing,* also is the creator of the *Printing Impressions Master Catalog,* a 516-page directory of all the printing equipment and supplies required for any printing process. The *Master Catalog* is the largest single publication ever produced for the industry.

In 1984, Borowsky coestablished the first Printing Hall of Fame with the Rochester Institute of Technology, one of America's leading technical universities. His sponsorship of the Hall underscores his firm's commitment to the standards of education that must be maintained in an industry that is governed by advances in new technologies.

Borowsky is a graduate of a printing school, created his own printing company as a teenager and during his illustrious career created nine new magazines including *TV Digest,* the forerunner of *TV Guide.* (Perhaps not-so-coincidentally, Borowsky pioneered the concept of selling magazines at supermarket checkout counters, and one of his publications, *Magazine & Bookseller,* is targeted to the merchandisers of such point-of-purchase publications.)

Well-known for his involvement in philanthropic activities, Borowsky has donated much time and money to causes that are ecumenical in nature and broad-based in scope. He has also established numerous scholarships at major institutions of learning.

It's perfectly consistent, therefore, that this guide to career opportunities in the printing and graphic arts industries has as its philosophical underpinning Borowsky's deep-seated interest in the welfare of young people, whom he believes will find this field rewarding and fulfilling.

Lewis R. Baratz, Ph.D., is professional services manager for a systems integration firm. He was a senior statistical analyst at Moody's Investors Service, and an executive assistant at American International Group. Trained as a music historian, Dr. Baratz was a Fulbright Scholar and is the author of *VGM's Guide to Temporary Employment* and the revision author of *Opportunities in Fitness Careers* and *Opportunities in Business Management Careers.* He is a columnist for *Exercise for Men Only,* the author of numerous articles on music history topics, and is currently working on a historical novel.

FOREWORD

Graphic communications. We used to call it printing, but new technologies have transformed the character of the graphic arts, making it an industry and career opportunity that is unlike any other. Computers, lasers, and twenty-first century electronics have transformed the skills that are needed from the rapidly growing work force. Graphic arts professionals are reconfiguring old patterns; they are creating more challenging jobs, and they are introducing new opportunities for people to grow and develop in their work. And the pace of this change isn't likely to slow down; to the contrary, it will accelerate. As it does, the graphic communications industries will experience an increased and on-going demand for people who must be recruited and trained to meet the needs of over 100,000 American businesses.

Printing in America has a rich and noble heritage, dating back to prerevolutionary times. Graphic communications today, however, is big business, ranking fourth in size among all U.S. manufacturing industries. More importantly, it's a growing industry. According to the U.S. Department of Commerce, the growth of commercial printing over the last ten years far outpaced the growth of manufacturing in general, *in every single state.* Looking ahead, the industry's demand for new people will continue its explosive pace, generating tens of thousands of new jobs every year well into the next century.

That's where you fit in. Job prospects for young people interested in the printing industry are excellent. Career opportunities in all areas of the graphic arts are varied, well-paying, and readily available.

Regardless of where you choose to live, it is impossible to think of a world without print, or a community without one—or several —printers.

This book has been written to help you explore career opportunities that are available in printing. If your interests are in management, an abundance of educational opportunities exist to prepare you for the complex challenges of running a communications business. If you like to sell, you'll find the competitive nature of print sales to be both thrilling and rewarding. If you're production oriented, the graphic arts offers enormous technological challenges. And, if you like science, you'll take interest in the printing industry's leadership position in being environmentally safe, aware, and responsive.

In reading this foreword, you have taken the first step along the path to an exciting career in graphic communications. Printing is an industry that offers a challenging, financially rewarding future that can be yours...simply for the taking.

> I. Gregg Van Wert
> President
> National Association of Printers and Lithographers

CHAPTER 1

THE HISTORY AND PRESENT IMPORTANCE OF PRINTING

If you're looking for a career, you've come to the right place. The U.S. printing industry is the largest such industry in the world. Printing is among the nation's foremost industries in general, encompassing both the government and private sectors. Gross receipts totaled over $100 billion (in current dollars) in 1990, second only to a half-dozen other manufacturing industries, with year-end 1996 sales exceeding $116 billion.

Printing is the largest manufacturing industry in several states. In Florida, for example, industry revenues for 1996 were in excess of $9 *billion,* with projected increases of up to 13 percent. According to the Printing Industries of Maryland, the state-wide payroll is approximately $600 million a year, paid to over 28,000 employees, most of whom earn an hourly wage above many other industries.

The printing industry is not just the number of presses churning out endless quantities of pages of printed matter. The U.S. Department of Commerce calls it the "Printing, Publishing and Allied Industries" (Standard Industry Code Major Group 27) and breaks the industry down into several distinct components.

Approximately 1,537,700 people were employed in the composite industry in the United States during the mid-1990s. In Canada, printing is that nation's fourth largest employer, with some

75,000 workers, producing over $9 billion in sales, and generating another $8 billion in other sectors of Canada's economy.

COMPONENTS OF THE PRINTING INDUSTRY[1]

The largest component in dollar volume is the newspaper industry (SIC Code 2711), with over 9,000 domestic newspapers and a payroll of more than $1.5 billion. Newspapers took in over $11 billion in sales and another $38 billion in advertising in 1995 and 1996, with some 60 million newspapers sold each day. Next is commercial printing (SIC Codes 2751–2759), with some 56,000 plants engaged in printing every description of printed matter, including advertising materials. Another major component of the industry is engaged in printing packages of all kinds, from metal cans to plastic bottles to folding cartons. It has been estimated that about 200,000 people work in 12,000 package printing plants. Business Forms (SIC Code 2761), Greeting Cards (SIC Code 2771), Typesetting (SIC Code 2791), and other subareas of the industry account for additional millions of the domestic payroll. Other industry components include magazine publishing, with more than 900 new titles added in 1996, book publishing and manufacture, and printing of such diverse items as gift wraps, wallpaper, and vinyl floor coverings.

An important branch is what is called by government statisticians "Trade Services," a generic term that serves all other components. These establishments include typesetters, platemakers, color separations producers, bookbinders, and related services. There are over 3,000 such plants in the United States employing about 180,000 people.

---

[1]Canadian statistics courtesy of the Canadian Printing Industry Association

So, you see, the printing industry is a diversified effort, a major force in the economies of North America, and a fertile ground for career planning. The industry as a whole employs about 1.6 million people in about 100,000 plants nationwide. The annual payroll of the printing industry, with all its subdivisions and classes, exceeds $38 billion annually.

Although these figures by themselves are impressive, even more impressive is the fact that about 80 percent of the 100,000 U.S. plants employ fewer than 20 persons. This means that printing is essentially a small-business enterprise. There are printing plants in every corner of the country—there is probably one just around the corner from where you live!

In addition to these bare facts and figures, understand that printing and publishing is one of the most progressive of all U.S. industries, deeply involved in new electronic and technological developments. These developments have application in the three phases of printing: *pre-press,* which is the preparation of materials for printing; *press,* which is the actual application of ink to paper; and *post-press,* which includes folding, binding, and trimming printed pages into books, magazines, newspapers, and pamphlets.

Computer technology is employed in the printing industry in many different ways. For example, in preparing text matter for the press, the writer nowadays has only to type the copy on an ordinary typewriter keyboard linked to a computer, and then punch a key. The computer will "read" the copy and format it, that is, divide it into evenly spaced columns, decide when and how to hyphenate at the end of the line, and deliver the finished copy in the form of a sheet of film or a "hard copy" sheet of paper. Electronic imaging technology is among the fastest-growing and farthest-reaching elements of the modern computing energy, with hundreds of hardware and software firms bringing out new scanning and imaging products every month. Indeed, as government agencies scramble to comply with the Federal Paperwork Reduction Act of 1995, and with businesses converting to the more efficient "paperless office environment," more and more career opportunities open in optical data transmission and storage, which in some instances compete with the more traditional printing industry, as exemplified by the advent of the electronic magazine.

Nonetheless, the computer has saved at least six steps, some of which could be accomplished in the past only by skilled workers putting in many hours. Even in matters of judgment and quality control, instrumentation has taken over some of the duties of skilled, experienced people. The density of a dot of colored ink makes an important difference in the fidelity of color printing. Formerly, this could be judged by a skilled press operator—the more skilled and experienced, the better—who then made adjustments to the ink fountain of the press to bring up or down the amount of ink deposited on the paper. This is now done in many plants by a *densitometer,* an instrument for reading the density of ink across the entire face of the printed sheet. Its readings are linked to the ink fountain, and adjustments are made automatically and continuously during the press run.

Despite these and many other space-age developments, the caliber of personnel in the printing industry remains high. Both labor and management are interested in maintaining a skilled and well-paid work force. Competition among employees is keen, perhaps due to the fact that the quality of the finished product is directly related to the motivation of the individual. As the saying goes, doctors bury their mistakes, and lawyers may argue themselves out of theirs, but printers must live with theirs for as long as the printed page survives. Thus, we see good reason for the special care and pride of the craft that exists in the printing industry.

Ink itself has undergone transformation in the past few years as new environmental regulations and industry response has put hundreds of chemists to work developing better quality inks. Indeed, energy-efficiency, concern for the environment, and high competition have yielded faster presses and created thousands of job for equipment designers and engineers.

EARNINGS

According to government statistics, average hourly wages in the printing industry are higher than the average for all manufacturing. In recent years, wages have risen due to greater competition for workers. According to the U.S. Bureau of Labor Statistics, the printing and publishing industry added 6,000 jobs in June 1997 alone. Yet as the pool of entry-level workers continues to shrink, the skills needed for these jobs have gotten increasingly complex. The average hourly earnings in June 1990 were $11.15 per hour as compared to $14.05 by early 1996.

Turnover among employees is less than the national average. Another important factor in the health of the American printing industry, and one that is not so easily measured, is the attainment in the United States of higher and higher educational levels among the population as a whole. The more educated a population, the more interest there is in the printed word, making for a growing demand. Related to this is the informal adoption of English as a "universal" language of international commerce and science, affecting favorably the export of English-language magazines, books, and newspapers.

As it stands today, the printing industry affords a great many career opportunities. Yet this is only a beginning. As we saw before, printing is undergoing change as technological developments introduce new methods and machines almost daily. These new machines, many of them, are not just "new and improved," they are sometimes totally new concepts, changing the way things have been done for centuries. These changes will bring about the elimination of some jobs, of course, but the net effect will be to raise the standards of skill and competence among all employees Thus, opportunities will grow for intelligent, adaptable, and motivated people. They will find a place in the graphic arts industry. In subsequent chapters, we'll take a more detailed look at the industry and its component parts.

A SHORT HISTORY OF PRINTING

Maybe you never thought about it this way, but printing is a technology whose primary purpose is to keep a record. From the earliest days of prehistory, when cave dwellers scratched their picture symbols on the walls of their caves, people have been obsessed with the need to put it on the record: How many buffalo were bagged in today's hunt? How many stocks were traded on Wall Street?

Now, a scratch or a painting on a cave wall is one way to get a message across, but it *is* limited. After all, only a handful of people can squeeze into a cave at any one time to view a pictograph. So the next step was clay and stone tablets, which could be distributed and stored—up to a point. Then came papyrus and then vellum, the specially processed skins of animals called parchment. On each of these substrates, the text of the message had to be laboriously hand-lettered by rows of scribes, monks, and other well-motivated workers. Still, the message was not getting out to a wide-enough audience, and the costs associated with assembling books and manuscripts were extreme. What was needed was a method of reproducing the message many times over and then distributing it to a wide readership: printing.

Printing requires a cheap and abundant surface to print on, a system of movable type to compose the message, and a printing press. Only in the past one hundred years or so have all the elements needed to print in *volume* fallen into place.

The Chinese invented paper, a cheap and abundant surface, and, about a thousand years before fifteenth-century German aristocrat Johannes Gutenberg made his important contribution, they also invented movable wooden type and a printing press of sorts. But the Chinese language is complex, with hundreds of different characters, and because of this, printing in China never advanced to any significant degree. It remained for Gutenberg to reinvent movable type during the 1400s, this time with metal instead of wood. But, in contrast to the Chinese, Gutenberg had only to contend with three dozen letters and numbers in the German alphabet. So his efforts succeeded, and books began to flood Europe to satisfy an unquenchable thirst for knowledge among people who were just emerging from the Middle Ages.

Printing presses sprung up throughout European capitals at the height of the Renaissance and early Baroque eras. In addition to the written word, printers began to refine music type as well as illustrative engravings necessitated by the advents of humanism and naturalism, and also improvements in architecture, pedagogy, and the early illustrative encyclopedias. Major centers of printing included Lyons, in France; the diligent press of Platin, also known as Plantijn, in Antwerp; the Vatican and other Italian presses; and Amsterdam, where printers improved the engraving process and freely "borrowed," translated, and undertook the publication of controversial (banned) books and pamphlets. Finally, to round out the picture, in the late 1800s, Ottmar Mergenthaler, a German immigrant in the United States, invented a machine that automatically cast molten lead into lines of type, eliminating the slow, laborious task of setting type by hand, letter by letter. He called it the Linotype machine, and printing has grown by leaps and bounds ever since.

UNDERSTANDING THE OPPORTUNITIES

The printing industry affords opportunities for many diverse skills and talents. If your abilities lie in the area of facts and figures, you may belong in the front office—as an estimator, cost accountant, or production scheduling coordinator. If you have an outgoing personality and are comfortable with people, you might find fulfillment in the sales department. If you're "good with your hands," stripping and platemaking require a delicate touch and steady nerves. Persons with mechanical skills would do well in the pressroom or bindery. Industrial engineers and equipment designers are needed to produce new machines to increase productivity and lower costs. Creative people will find that the printing industry is *always* seeking good designers, layout and paste-up artists, and creative idea people. Procurement and compliance officers are needed to handle government and environmental issues and to submit competitive proposals for large corporate and government contract bids. If you're a technology person or a good web designer, there's the computer side of the business, with its need for people who are both scientific and artistic. Indeed, a skilled computer graphics designer can basically write his or her own ticket. So you see, for centuries the printing industry has been a magnet for business-minded people, technicians, craftspeople, and designers

Printing is indeed a pervasive industry. You and I come into contact with some kind of printing every day and minute of our lives. Consider some of the things besides newspapers and magazines that are printed: money, marriage licenses, laws, wet paint signs, product labels, auto registration tags, shoe sizes, greeting cards, and, yes, even oranges! As we have seen, printing is one of the largest industries in America. This is because every enterprise, large or small, must be supported by some kind of printed matter. Invoices and statements help bring in money; sales brochures help sell the product; stock offerings fuel expansions; and plans for an expansion are put down on paper before a stone is turned.

In addition to the sheer volume of printing, with its many opportunities for a worthwhile career, printing offers something additional. When you are in printing, you are in the vanguard of American business, industry, or education. Riding on the front bumper of the earthship Enterprise, so to speak, you, as a printer crewperson, are privileged to receive insights into the way things work in the world of American and international business.

Benjamin Franklin, the patron saint of printing in America, summed up the essence of career planning two hundred years ago: "Human felicity is produced not so much by great pieces of good fortune that seldom happen, as by little advantages that occur every day."

UNDERSTANDING PRINTING

Before you embark upon your career in printing, it would be wise to acquire an understanding of the various ways in which words and pictures are put on paper today. This understanding of the basics of printing will help you no matter which aspect of the industry you decide to enter. A list of printing terms and their definitions appears in the glossary (Appendix E) in the back of this book.

First, let's have a look at the various methods of printing:

- Lithography
- Letterpress
- Flexography
- Gravure
- Screen printing

Lithography

The *lithographic* method of printing is by far the most common, accounting for about one-half of all U.S. printing. It is also known as *planographic printing, offset lithography,* and the *photo offset process.* This method of printing has become popular only in this century. Its simplicity has fostered the growth of thousands of instant printing centers in the United States. It is based on a simple natural phenomenon: Water and oil repel each other.

Here's how the process works: A thin sheet of metal is coated with an oil-based substance called an *emulsion.* The metal sheet, or plate, is placed in contact with a film, called a *negative,* on which an image has been photographically developed. The portions of the image that are to be printed are so dense that light cannot pass through them. Portions of the image that are *not* to be printed are left clear on the negative. A bright light is turned on briefly. Light strikes the emulsion coating on the plate wherever the negative has been left clear. The light causes a chemical reaction in the emulsion. Where the images exist on the negative, no light can pass through, and the emulsion beneath it remains undisturbed.

The plate is then removed from contact with the negative and washed in a chemical solution. The solution attacks the portion of the plate where light was permitted to pass and the emulsion is washed away, leaving the metal bare. Where light did not strike the emulsion, the solution has no effect, and the emulsion remains and hardens.

The plate is then strapped to a cylinder on the printing press. As it revolves, it is first coated with a thin application of water. The water will readily wet the bare metal. It will be repelled by the emulsion image left on the plate. As the plate continues turning on the cylinder, it comes into contact with an inked roller. You should understand that printing ink is an oil-based product. Since water and oil repel each other, no ink is deposited on the wet plate in the blank areas. However, the ink readily adheres to the emulsion-coated areas.

The plate cylinder now comes into contact with a rubber blanket cylinder and the image is transferred. As the blanket cylinder revolves, it next comes into contact with the printing paper, and the image is again transferred, this time to the paper. Because the image is transferred twice, it is "right reading" on the plate and on the paper (meaning reversed as to left and right). It is "wrong reading" on the blanket cylinder. This transferring of the image from plate to blanket to paper is why the process is called offset printing.

Letterpress

Letterpress printing, also called *relief printing,* is the oldest of the printing processes. Whereas in offset lithography a thin metal plate is used, letterpress printing employs a much thicker, rigid metal plate or metal type. The plate has two surfaces—a raised surface, which is the original thickness of the plate, and an undercut surface. The undercutting of the plate is accomplished by etching the plate with acid. Areas that are to be printed are "stopped" by a gummy substance that resists acid. Those areas not to be printed are left bare. The plate is then immersed in a powerful acid bath.

The bare metal is eaten away by the acid, to a depth where the ink roller cannot reach the valleys. The plate is then washed clean and the acid resist removed. The plate is then strapped to the bed of the press or to a curved cylinder. As the press operates, the plate is brought into contact alternately with an ink roller and the paper to be printed. The plate picks up ink on its raised surface and deposits it on the paper. In letterpress, the image is wrong reading on the plate and right reading on the paper.

Until the later 1800s, letterpress was the most widely used process in the production of newspapers, magazines, books, and other volume products. In the United States and other industrial nations, offset printing has supplanted letterpress in most, if not all, these applications. However, letterpress is still common throughout Latin America and the Developing World.

Flexography

Flexography is a printing process related to letterpress, inasmuch as it employs a raised printing surface, which is inked and applied to the paper. When you use a rubber stamp, you are using the basic elements of the flexographic process: you apply wet ink to raised flexible type and then press the type against a sheet of paper. The difference is that flexography employs a flexible plate, usually made of rubber or photopolymer, and specially prepared inks are used. Applications include packaging materials such as cardboard and plastic films.

Gravure

Gravure printing is similar to letterpress printing in that a relatively thick and rigid metal plate is used. Ink is applied to the plate or type with a roller, and the plate is then pressed against a sheet of paper. The main difference is that instead of being raised, the image is *dug out* of the surface of the plate. (The process is also called *intaglio* printing, which means incised carving.) Ink is then applied to the entire surface of the gravure plate and wiped away on a roll of special paper. After the wiping, ink remains trapped in the grooves of the plate. The plate is then pressed against the paper with enormous pressure. The ink is absorbed by the paper and the image reproduced on its surface. In gravure printing, the image is also wrong reading on the plate.

Gravure technology has changed rapidly in the past few years owing to computer software and electronic imaging techniques. Conferences and journals dedicated to the subject are laden with advanced technical breakthroughs and procedures that challenge students and seasoned masters alike.

Applications for gravure printing are large quantities of books, magazines, catalogs, and Sunday supplements, in which the pictures require better-than-average fidelity in color, such as art reproductions. A related process, called engraving, employs the same techniques as gravure but on a smaller scale. Applications include money, letterheads, and all sorts of documents and certificates.

Screen Printing

The fifth process, *screen printing,* is also called porous printing or silk screening. It employs a cloth screen stencil on which an image has been drawn by hand, or photographically exposed. Those portions of the image that are to be printed are left clear on the screen. Those portions not to be printed are stopped by an impermeable resist (a substance that cannot be penetrated). The screen is placed in contact with the paper, ink is allowed to flow freely over the surface of the screen, and then a squeegee is wiped across the screen, forcing the ink through the silk screen mesh onto the paper. Applications for the process include outdoor posters, point-of-purchase advertising materials, and other products normally printed in limited quantities.

Other Printing Processes

Two new printing processes that are now in general use are *ink jet printing* and *electrostatic printing.* In the first process, tiny droplets of ink are propelled onto the surface of the paper. There is no physical contact between plate and paper, as there is in all other

printing processes. Electrostatic printing deposits colored parti-
cles of resin that are held in place by a magnetic force and then
fused to the paper to form an image.

WHERE ARE THE JOBS?

For centuries, printing technology remained fairly stable, with
little or no change over the years. Only in recent times have any significant changes occurred, and these have been mostly in the pre-
press phase. A graphic artist employed in the 1940s could still hold
down a similar position in the 1960s with little or no retraining.

However, in the past few decades, many technical jobs have
changed drastically. In some positions, such as those in the preparation phase, an old-timer would be totally lost. The stripping
department, the typesetting department, the camera room, and the
platemaking section would be nearly unrecognizable. Likewise,
the older printer would not see the familiar banks of linotype
machines and wouldn't smell and feel the heat of molten white
metal.

But don't let these drastic changes discourage you. The important fact that emerges from the upheaval going on in the printing
industry is summed up in one word: opportunity. Whenever there is
change, new avenues for progress open up. These new roads will
be traveled by informed, well-trained, and competent craftspersons. In addition to craftspersons, printing will have pressing needs
for engineers, scientists, computer technicians, accountants, sales-
people, copy editors, and artists. To each of these positions the
applicant must bring a flexible mind and be able and *willing* to try
something different, no matter how radical it may seem.

The rewards are quite generous. Because the industry requires
such a diverse set of skills, it is willing to pay for them. Newspaper
production employees, for example, are among the highest paid

blue-collar workers in the nation, averaging in 1989 more than $11 per hour, and approximately $14 an hour in 1996. The average for printers as a whole is similarly high, with even higher wages for unionized workers. The segments of the printing industry that are currently growing, and which therefore offer the greatest opportunities, are the pre-press and post-press phases. However, it must be understood that in spite of a net growth, some jobs in these phases are being eliminated because of the efficient use of new high-technology equipment. The opportunities occur because of first, the overall growth of printing, estimated at about 4 percent per year into the early 1990s; and second, the substitution of new skills to take the place of the phased-out skills.

If a new stripping machine cuts down on the number of strippers employed in a plant, it also requires at least one new employee to operate the machine. The new employee does not have to know how to use a razor blade or scribe a clean line, but that person does have to know how to get the most out of a sophisticated piece of electronic equipment.

The job opportunities are *not* in Linotype machine operating, stereotype making, plate engraving, proof press operating, or page lockup—all jobs associated with letterpress printing. The best and brightest opportunities lie in the fields most affected by technological progress: photocomposition, automated picture scanning, electronic color proofing, computer-assisted page makeup, computerized text editing, electronic stripping, and automated platemaking, along with business skills such as computer-based accounting, pricing, and estimating, to name a few.

Although the printing industry is huge, it is made up of over 100,000 different firms, averaging about $1.5 million each in annual receipts. Eighty percent of the printing firms in the United States can be classified as small businesses employing fewer than 20 persons, with the owners and managers actively involved in the day-to-day operations of the company. The newcomer to the field has a clear-cut choice: cast your lot with the big firms where you can expect to find a niche for a specialized skill, or go for the smaller firms where you can realize your potential in broader management abilities. Each choice offers advantages and disadvantages that should be weighed carefully before you make a decision.

It should be emphasized that a choice is necessary. If you seek a position with a large or small printing establishment, you should tailor your job seeking to the ultimate goal. A campaign to win a job as a manager trainee in a tightly controlled small firm must necessarily emphasize your abilities as an all-around achiever with broad knowledge of all aspects of the printing business. If you're aiming to join the world of big business in a major corporation, your best avenue of approach is to offer a specialized skill and go from there.

In subsequent chapters in this book, we'll examine each of the jobs in printing and allied trades in greater detail. Then you can make up your own mind where you belong in the space-age graphic arts industry.

CHAPTER 2

OPPORTUNITIES IN PRINTING

Printing is such a diverse industry that you are well advised to become acquainted not only with the geographical locations of the best job opportunities, but also with the various career alternatives existing in each component of the printing industry: newspapers, commercial printers, book manufacturers, trade shops, and others. While most components of the industry are expected to grow into the early twenty-first century, some segments will grow at a faster rate than others. In the 1980s, the printing industry was one of only five manufacturing industries that showed net gains in employment.

Here is a brief description of each component, with tips on how you might relate each of them to your own career planning or job-seeking program. If any of the terms in these descriptions are unclear to you, check the glossary in the back of this book.

NEWSPAPER PRINTING

There are over 1,520 daily newspapers in the United States producing some 50 million copies of newspapers every day. The larger dailies are located in the large population centers of the nation. Daily newspapers operate their own printing plants, and the majority of production workers are members of a union.

Another 35 million copies are printed by the nation's 7,915 weekly newspapers every week.

Most weeklies are printed by commercial printing plants under contract with the weekly newspaper publisher. Such plants may, and frequently do, print more than one weekly, some as many as a dozen or more. Geographically, weeklies are located in all sections of the United States, coinciding roughly with the population centers of the country. Employees of weeklies and the plants that print them are not as tightly organized as the dailies.

The jobs in newspaper printing run the gamut of all graphic arts occupations, from phototypesetting to laser beam scanner operator. However, although some small, primarily rural, newspapers may still require the services of hot metal typesetting machine operators, such positions have been virtually phased out as typesetting has entered the high-technology world of word processors, remote VDTs, and high-speed printers. The positions of electrotyper and stereotyper, occupations that are associated with letterpress printing of newspapers, are now fundamentally archaic.

COMMERCIAL PRINTING

There are about 50,000 commercial printing plants in the United States, many of them with 20 employees or fewer. Commercial printing employs close to 600,000 workers in jobs as varied as those of any industry in America. Total gross receipts of this component were some $53 billion in 1990, and over $70 billion in 1996. The industry is widely dispersed, with plants employing 50 or more people in every state and nearly every county. However, the larger printing plants tend to be concentrated in or near centers of industrial activity. About two-thirds of the plants are located along the Eastern Seaboard from New England through the Mid-

Atlantic states. About 20 percent are located in the West, and the remainder are scattered through the nation's heartland.

Your job opportunities in printing are greater in the commercial printing field, because commercial printers tend to adopt innovations in production techniques more readily than the other segments of the printing industry. This is because of the pressure of competition and the more modest investment required to implement a new idea in the relatively smaller commercial plant. These new ideas require people with new skills never before seen in the graphic arts. Some examples are digital press make ready system operator, color proof scanner operator, densitometer evaluator, and phototype keyboard operator.

The age of information is a present reality. The old ways of doing things in the pressroom must give way to newer techniques aimed at increasing production levels and lowering costs, if the printer is to stay competitive. Not only must printers increase their aggressiveness in the marketplace, they also must be flexible enough in their thinking and in the structure of their organizations to adapt to the exotica of modern electronics, film science, and satellites—all of which adds up to many employment opportunities.

PACKAGE PRINTING PLANTS

A large but relatively unsung segment of the printing industry is package printing. The products of this component include plastic film and foil bags, cartons, tags and labels, plastic and metal containers, wrappers, and many other packaging materials and products. Package printing is done by flexography, gravure, sheetfed offset, and rotary letterpress, the latter being used mainly for tags and labels.

Flexographic printing is a $28- to $30-billion market, much of it devoted to package printing. The gravure segment is a $6.2-billion market, a significant portion of which is devoted to package printing. According to the Flexographic Technical Association, there are about 200,000 persons employed in the industry. There are about 4,500 flexographic printing plants in the United States, most of which are concentrated in the large population centers.

MAGAZINE PUBLISHING AND PRINTING

Magazine publishing has experienced growth in the past five years, registering gains in both circulation and advertising receipts. Of the three major groups (consumer, business, and farm publications), consumer magazines are showing the most promising growth. Gains in advertising and circulation revenue result in increased opportunities in the printing side of the industry.

In an effort to keep circulation of printed magazines up, more than 900 new titles were added in 1996, despite fierce competition from electronic magazines available via subscription or free on the Internet. Nonetheless, the growth rate forecast for the magazine publishing industry is consistent with the growth rate predicted for the entire graphic arts industry. In 1983, periodicals revenues amounted to over $11 billion and the industry employed about 85,000 people, over 16,000 of whom were production workers. By 1991 total periodical receipts had swelled to over $33 billion.

Some of the high-priced, slick magazines are printed by gravure, a process that allows the highest quality reproduction of color art and is also capable of the long runs needed to print in large volume. Offset lithography is used for the production of publications with shorter runs and less exacting color requirements.

BOOK PRINTING

The U.S. book printing industry is composed of about 1,000 establishments employing about 33,000 production workers. Receipts in recent years have amounted to $4 billion annually with a growth rate that approximates that of the printing industry as a whole. The greatest growth in book printing has come from the production of paperbound books, as opposed to the more expensive hardbounds.

The book printing industry benefits from the same factors that are spurring growth in magazine publishing—increased literacy in the population as a whole, the increasing adoption of English as a second language among the nations of the world, and the general stability of raw materials, prices, and availability. The jobs in book publishing are concentrated in New York, Boston, and Philadelphia, and in the Great Lakes area and the West Coast. The predominant printing method for books is lithography, which amounts to about 85 percent. Competition, however, is coming from computer-generated books that are "desktop-published," quickly and inexpensively, with visual results that are a far cry from the professional quality that ensues from the established printing press.

BUSINESS FORMS MANUFACTURE

There are about 800 plants engaged in the manufacture of business forms, a specialized industry requiring special-purpose printing presses and highly trained personnel. The industry employs about 35,000 production workers, operating mainly lithographic printing presses, although some plants are switching to "dry" offset, a letterpress version employing polymer printing plates.

Several factors are involved in gauging the growth of the industry. Chief among these is the proliferation of computer technology in all levels of business. Computers are prodigious consumers of printed forms, in sets or single sheets. However, modern technology has also created new ways of storing and retrieving data directly from computer memory, making unnecessary the filing (and printing) of many tons of printed paper. The demand for printed forms is expected, nevertheless, to continue at its present high levels through the middle of the decade.

In addition to offset lithography, the industry is experimenting with new methods such as ink jet printing and electrostatic printing, as described in Chapter 1.

OTHER PRINTING ESTABLISHMENTS

The other segments of the printing industry provide considerable opportunities for printing careers when taken as a whole, but in their respective areas the jobs are less numerous than in those just described. Let's review each of them.

Greeting Card Printing

The greeting card industry has been growing at a steady rate for many years, but several factors combine to limit the number of job opportunities for printers. First, there is the essential fact that 80 percent of the total U.S. output is produced by about four companies. Although the number of greeting card companies has increased over the past five years, to over $6 billion in sales in 1996, employment declined by 1,000 workers. The majority of greeting card establishments have fewer than 20 employees, not all of them involved in production. Many greeting card publishers farm out their printing requirements to commercial printers.

The vast majority of greeting cards are printed by lithographic printing, augmented by such processes as die stamping, die cutting, embossing, converting, and flocking, all of which require special skills not ordinarily found in pressrooms and commercial establishments.

Quick Printing Shops

Quick printing shops have proliferated in the past few years. The main reason for their success has been the development of "smart" machines that require little or no training or experience of their operators. Printing plates of metal or paper are exposed and processed in automatically controlled platemakers. Small duplicating presses are easily operated by personnel with no prior experience, printing "by the numbers." The nature of the work done by quick printing shops is, of course, uncomplicated, usually in a single ink color on basic paper stock and usually supplied flat or without complicated folds and finishing.

If you are seeking a career leading to the achievement of master printer status, you will not find that opportunity in quick printing shops, although many craftspersons are finding business success as owners of such shops.

In-Plant Printing

This segment of the printing industry is not as easily identified as the other components. Most large organizations have their own in-house "captive" shop on the premises, producing a wide range of printed matter, from company newsletters to assembling instructions to point-of-purchase displays in full color. Finding jobs in these firms is not as easy as consulting your local telephone directory, but with some 30,000 shops, there are plenty of job opportunities. In-plant printing shops also exist in companies outside of manufacturing, such as insurance companies, mail-order firms, retail stores, and religious and other charitable organizations.

In-plant printing equipment represents every type used in commercial printing, including the most sophisticated. Because large firms have the resources to afford the latest state-of-the-art technology, in-plant printing shops tend to be well equipped and well managed—sometimes better even than commercial shops of comparable size. Thus, the opportunities are often greater in in-plant shops for personal growth and technical advancement.

Trade Shops

This component of the printing industry includes such establishments as typesetters, color separators, platemakers, and bookbinders. These shops provide services to printers amounting to about $1.9 billion.

Trade shops are widely dispersed throughout the U. S. population centers. With employment numbering about 20,000, they represent promising opportunities for the newcomer to the graphic arts.

OPPORTUNITIES SUMMARIZED

In reviewing the opportunities afforded by the printing industry, you should bear in mind that not all jobs in printing have strictly

to do with printing. The printing industry needs management and executive personnel as much as any other industry. It also needs good people in accounting, sales, computer technology, production planning, estimating, and graphic design.

CHAPTER 3

ADMINISTRATIVE JOBS IN PRINTING

Before investigating the individual jobs in printing, it is a good idea to become acquainted with some of the presses and other equipment used in printing. There are three basic configurations of printing presses: *platen, cylinder,* and *rotary,* irrespective of the printing process being employed. However, platen and cylinder presses are no longer used on a widespread basis. More than one kind of press may be used in a printing process. For example, gravure may be done on rotary presses; letterpress may be done with all three types.

Platen presses are those with a flat bed on which the type form rests. The type is inked with a roller (mechanically or by hand), and the paper is pressed against the wet type form. The paper may be fed by hand or mechanically.

Cylinder presses, which may be horizontal or vertical, also support the type form on a flat bed, and the type is inked in the same manner as on a platen press. A cylinder is then rolled over the inked type, carrying the paper with it, and the impression is made. Grippers close and open as the cylinder travels over the type form, alternately grasping and releasing the paper at the delivery end of the press.

Rotary presses include *web presses.* They are used to print newspapers, magazines, catalogs, and books in large volume. Instead of a flat bed and a type form, two cylinders act in opposition, one being the form cylinder and the other the impression cylinder. Instead of a flat type form, a metal plate is curved to fit the radius of the cylinder and locked in place.

Presses may also be classified as *sheetfed* and *webfed.* As its name implies, a sheetfed press sends the paper through one sheet at a time. In a webfed press, paper in a continuous roll, called a *web,* is passed between the cylinders to make the impression. Web presses are capable of printing on both sides of the web of paper, drying, folding, cutting, and assembling pages at the delivery end of the press.

PRINTING EQUIPMENT

Although printing presses still conform to traditional design and function, the same cannot be said of the other equipment in the printing plant. The areas that are undergoing the most drastic changes are typesetting and imaging, both of them in the pre-press phase of the printing operation.

In a nutshell, the changes that are occurring result in less emphasis on craft among employees and greater emphasis on technological skills. With the aid of computers, typesetting has become more of an automated process. Now, the typesetter needs to learn how to tend a computerized photocompositor, learning to look for potential trouble spots by observing its functioning, and performing the tasks necessary to keep it operating reliably. In other words, while the typesetters of today still need to know typefaces, they now need to add to their body of knowledge the intricacies of printed circuits, relays, and microchips. In the area of imaging, there are now machines that can take over the major share of the work of preparing materials ready for printing.

This is called pre-press technology. Machines now proof color separations on a video screen, eliminating the laborious task of printing each color separately on a proof press. Electronic pre-press systems integrate text and graphics to produce plate-ready films. Automatic scanners eliminate the camera work previously necessary to screen halftone negatives and plates, some with laser beams that are far more sensitive to variations of light and dark than the camera lens.

Another avenue we should mention here is document imaging and *optical character resolution, OCR* in computer lingo. These technologies are enabling businesses and individuals to mass "print" virtually anything for which they have hard copy. By converting text documents, photos, presswork, or just about anything on paper, to an electronic medium ("digitized"), the images can be stored, manipulated, adjoined to other images, and so forth. But the results are only as good as the laser or bubble-jet printer used, and although electronic document technology is a complex and highly technical profession, it cannot afford the high quality work of the modern printing press.

JOB DESCRIPTIONS

The jobs selected for description in this and the next two chapters cover every aspect of the printing industry. They are divided into *Administrative, Pre-Press,* and *Pressroom and Bindery.* Some highly specialized jobs, such as operators of densitometers, automated stripping machines, and automatic make ready machines, have not been included because they are adjuncts to the jobs of press operator and stripper, differing only in their methods of accomplishing the same result. Note that in some job descriptions, you may find words that are unfamiliar. These may be defined in the glossary at the back of the book.

The salaries and hourly rates given at the end of each job description are based on national averages and means, taking into account such variables as geographic location, the experience and length of service of the employee, and the size of the firm. The printing industry is one of the tougher industries to benchmark salaries owing to absence of systematic national data. Thus, the figures given are furnished as a general guide. There can be exceptional circumstances that would change the rates to a higher or lower figure than those given.

JOB OPPORTUNITIES

The administrative staff of a printing firm differs little from the administrative staff of any business. The main concern of printing executives, in an equipment-intensive industry such as printing, is the acquisition and operation of the latest and most efficient printing presses and auxiliary equipment. Clerical, accounting, and personnel departments would be structured and staffed as they would in any business. The following positions, however, are unique to the printing industry.

Printing Sales Manager

Sales managers are most commonly employed by large commercial printers to coordinate and supervise the efforts of the sales staff. They recruit, train, and supervise the work of the sales representatives in selling the services of the plant. They establish goals, quotas, and territories and analyze sales statistics to formulate policy and to determine customer needs and requirements. They coordinate with the production department, altering sales strategies as necessary to keep the plant operating at maximum capacity, and bring to the attention of potential customers any new technological capabilities the firm may offer.

Sales managers are responsible for administering the compensation of the sales representatives who report to them. They arrange technical training sessions for the sales staff to acquaint them with new printing developments and prepare periodic sales reports showing volume and potential. The sales manager's salary and earnings may vary widely from firm to firm, from $35,000 to $200,000 annually, depending on the volume of business.

To enter the job market as an upwardly-mobile printing sales manager, an undergraduate degree in business with marketing skills is recommended. A solid knowledge of the industry standards, terminology, and technology is essential, and entrant managers should begin to study for an MBA early on in their careers.

Printing Sales Representative

A member of the sales staff of a commercial printer, business forms printer, or magazine and book printer as well as trade shops and binderies, the printing sales representative visits business establishments to solicit business for printing. He or she interviews purchasing personnel and quotes prices from a schedule or obtains a price from the printing firm's estimator. Printing sales representatives explain technical matters, such as typesetting requirements, paper weight and quality, binding materials, and the various methods of reproduction that the firm can offer. They contact prospects by following leads furnished by their management or generated through their own efforts by telephone or mail. They visit established customers regularly. They may prepare sales promotional letters and submit formal bids in writing on large orders. They work under a commission arrangement, or salary, or a combination of both.

Many of the larger firms have organized training programs. Some prefer to promote personnel into sales from within their inside service staff. These are people who know better than any new addition to the staff their plant's ability to produce specialized work. Compensation after training is usually salary plus commissions plus selling expenses. Total earnings often can vary from $25,000 to $75,000. In some cases, they may exceed $100,000 annually.

Printing Estimator

Most commercial and business forms printers must compete against each other for business, furnishing quotes on jobs before being awarded the order. Printing estimators draw upon their knowledge of printing and their experience to estimate costs of labor and materials in the printing and binding of advertising matter, magazines, books, and other printed products. The estimate is based on the specifications outlined on the request for a quotation.

Estimating requires knowledge of all aspects of the industry, from the price of paper and ink, to labor costs, to density factors, to overhead, overtime, and packaging costs. They examine the specs (specifications), including sketches or comprehensive layouts, and calculate unit and incremental costs, using labor and material pricing schedules prepared by them previously. They confer with department heads and production personnel to confirm their figures. They also may be required to estimate mailing weight and cost of mailing of finished product. Estimators must be able to use computer spreadsheets or other automated tools in their calculations, and be able to offer a wide variety of processes and options to clients. Salaries range from $30,000 to over $60,000 annually.

Advertising and Sales Promotion Manager

Newspapers, magazine and book publishers, and many large commercial printing firms employ an advertising and sales promotion manager. In some of the larger firms, the two jobs are separate. In the case of newspapers and periodical publishers, it is the product that is advertised and promoted. In the case of commercial printers, it is the printing service. The advertising manager plans and administers an advertising campaign in various advertising media such as radio, TV, and print publications. The sales promotion manager may be involved with point-of-purchase displays, trade exhibits, and publicity. The advertising and sales promotion manager is responsible for developing sales leads furnished to the sales department. He or she confers with other managers to develop sales strategies and campaigns, administers the advertising and sales promotion budget, and submits reports as required. Starting salaries range from $22,000 to $35,000, depending upon the size of the firm, with average salaries exceeding $40,000 for five years or more experience.

Purchasing Manager

All sizable printing firms employ a purchasing manager (or agent), who is the buyer for all raw materials and supplies and services required by the firm. Purchasing managers place orders for all raw materials, such as paper, all new and replacement machinery and equipment, and all supplies, such as ink and chemicals, used in the printing process. They review requisitions, and they interview vendors to obtain information concerning the product or service, such as the price, delivery and capability of the vendor. They estimate the value of the product or service from their own knowledge of the market. They may be called on to seek replacements or refunds for damaged or defective products. A purchasing manager may also approve bills for payment. Salaries can range from $30,000 to $60,000 annually.

Inventory Control Manager

All printing firms must keep control over supplies of raw material to prevent shortages during production runs. The larger printing establishments employ inventory control managers who keep records on ordering, receiving, storing, issuing, and shipping. They compile data from these records, arranged so that the availability of any item may be ascertained at a glance. They maintain a stock control record to show consumption rates, current market conditions, condition of items in storage, and other information required to make replenishment decisions. They compare catalog numbers and descriptions with actual items to verify the accuracy of requisitions and purchase orders. They periodically review their files to determine which items are not being used and recommend disposal when indicated. Since many firms employ computers to manage inventory stocks, an inventory control manager or clerk should be experienced in their operation. Salaries ranges from $18,000 to $40,000 annually.

Personnel Manager

All medium-sized and larger printing plants employ a personnel manager to supervise the employment activities of the firm. Personnel managers develop sources of qualified applicants for positions within the firm, conduct screening interviews, administer tests, and check references and background. They evaluate the applicant's experience and confer with department heads to establish the applicant's qualification for the position. They arrange for indoctrination interviews and trial-period hiring according to company policy. They keep records on employees' performance and recommend promotion, termination, and transfers as indicated. They conduct exit interviews and respond to requests from other firms for references. They analyze statistical data concerning work force functioning in general, making recommendations to company management for personnel policy changes as required. They may be responsible for vacation scheduling. Salaries may range from $30,000 to $80,000 annually, depending on the size of the firm.

Cost Accountant

Many printing firms require detailed information on costs that are not supplied by ordinary accounting methods. The cost accountant plans, implements, and directs cost finding and reporting systems to isolate, record, and determine unit costs of raw materials, supplies, and labor. Cost accountants analyze changes in product design, raw materials, overhead, manufacturing methods, or wages for their effect on production costs. They prepare reports comparing actual costs with standards for the industry as a whole. They supply management with reports that might indicate that changes are needed in pricing or production, and they make a special comparison of public utility rates and consumption, maintaining current data for use in establishing unit costs. They may be called on for appraisal of real property and capital equipment for tax purposes.

A degree in accounting is strongly recommended for this type of work. At a minimum, junior cost accountants should be adept at financial analysis, using computer spreadsheets. Salaries range from $25,000 to $40,000 annually.

Controller

Printing firms doing a large volume of business employ a controller who directs the financial affairs of the firm. Controllers prepare the financial analysis of operations for the guidance of management.

Controllers also establish economic objectives and policies for the company, in conference with management. They prepare reports that outline the company's financial position in areas of income, expenses, and earnings based on past, present, and future operations. They direct the preparation of budgets and financial forecasts and determine depreciation rates applied to capital equipment. They prepare government reports as required and advise management on adjustments to operations that could be desirable from a tax point of view. They advise management on insurance coverage against property losses and liability protection.

A controller is usually not a recent graduate. A minimum of a bachelor's degree in accounting and at least three years experience in general accounting or financial analysis is required in most cases. Salaries range from $35,000 to $90,000 annually, depending on the volume of business, demographics, and experience of the controller.

Public Relations Manager

Only the very largest printing firms employ a public relations manager or director. Unlike the advertising and sales promotion manager, the public relations manager is not involved in selling the product or service, but rather in creating and maintaining a favorable public image for the firm. Public relations managers place stories in print and electronic media about the company's accomplishments, programs, or point of view. They contact and confer with legislators and government officials to persuade them to enact or enforce legislation favorable to the company's interests. They serve as spokespersons for the company in times of increased public notice or a newsworthy event. They act as compliance officers to ensure that the inks and other materials used are environmentally sound. They prepare and distribute fact sheets, news releases, photographs, and tapes to press representatives. They also promote goodwill for the company by speeches, exhibits, and films about the company as well as tours of the plant, and they represent the company at public gatherings and social functions. Some may write proposals in response to open-bid requests from government agencies and private corporations for large, multi-million dollar orders. Salaries range from $25,000 to $75,000 annually, depending on the size of the firm.

Plant Superintendent

This management-level executive is found in all printing plants with more than one press in operation. Plant superintendents direct and coordinate, through subordinate supervisory personnel, all the activities involved in the production of printed matter. They must be knowledgeable in all phases of the company's production operations and the capabilities of each piece of machinery and equipment. They confer with management to establish quality control standards, develop budget and cost controls, and receive information on quantities, delivery dates, and specs of customer orders. They conduct hearings with plant personnel to settle grievances and listen to complaints. They confer with department heads to receive reports on the performance of department personnel. They may be involved in the hiring of production personnel, particularly those in key positions in the pressroom. Salaries ranges from $30,000 to over $100,000 annually, depending on the size of the firm.

CHAPTER 4

PRE-PRESS JOBS

The positions discussed in this chapter have to do with the steps necessary to prepare a job for the pressroom, including the original concept of the job, typesetting, preparing the art for the camera, stripping the flat, and making the plates. This phase of printing is undergoing the greatest amount of change as new processes and machines come on-line to streamline the printing process.

If you are planning a career in this phase, you should emphasize your technical skills, particularly in the field of computers and electronics. A clear understanding of these fields will be an invaluable aid to your progress. If you find an unfamiliar word in the job descriptions that follow, check for a definition in the glossary at the back of the book (See Appendix E).

According to the *Occupational Outlook Handbook* (1996 edition), compiled by the U.S. Department of Labor, there are some 169,000 pre-press workers in the United States today. Thirty-one thousand of these persons are employed as strippers and printers, another 22,000 as paste-up workers, 15,000 as camera operators, 13,000 as platemakers, 20,000 as typesetting and composing machine operators, and 18,000 as electronic pagination systems workers. The remaining professionals are involved in photo-engraving, lithographic machine operation, and other precision aspects of pre-press production. The best outlook for job growth is in the electronic sector of the industry, as clients become more sophisticated with desktop publishing, and turn over to printers their ideas in a nearly-complete diskette format that requires sophisticated manipulation rather than paper paste-up design from scratch.

POSITIONS IN COLD TYPE COMPOSITION

The term *cold type* refers to any method of type composition in which hot, molten metal is not involved. Cold-type printing processes are the most common in the United States today, thus job opportunities will be more numerous and varied in this field than in traditional areas associated with hot type. Some examples of cold-type composition are strike-on typewriter, photocomposition, and electronic or computer-assisted typesetting.

Varitype Operator

Varitype machines are found in some weekly newspapers; magazine, book, and publishing companies; and printing establishments. The operator types master copy on glossy paper stock, stencils, direct plates, and tracings having the appearance of a printed type. He or she plans the layout of page elements from rough visuals, determines size and style of type, sets horizontal and vertical spacing and margins, and calculates anticipated dimensions of copy to be enlarged or reduced.

The operator attaches gear to the platen to control spacing between lines and moves a lever to control spacing between characters. He or she sets stops to control the right margin and changes style and size of type by pressing a type-change key and turning the font from reserve to typing position. The operator also may draw decorative or illustrative designs on copy and may lay out and rule forms and charts using drafting tools. Salary is usually $10 per hour or more.

Phototypesetter Operator

This position is similar to that of photocomposing machine operator, except that the machine is operated by a keyboard instead of by perforated tapes. The operator loads a roll of photosensitive paper or film into a camera magazine, positions the magazine on the machine, and pulls a lever to open the exposure slot. She or he then starts the typesetting mechanism, turns a dial to select the lens, and adjusts a gear that selects the type size to magnify or reduce the matrix letter. The operator also controls exposure and light intensity and may distort images to widen or condense letters and create special effects. He or she then depresses keys on the keyboard to select individual letters and form words from photo mats to photographic paper or film, and then removes the photo-paper or film from the magazine for developing. The operator per-forms user maintenance on the machine as required. The usual salary is $13.75 or more an hour.

Electronic Typesetting Machine Operator

The electronic typesetter is one of a proliferating series of machines that use electronic and computer-assisted hardware to set, develop, and print type for a variety of applications in printing newspapers, magazines, and books. The operator sits at the key-board of the machine and auxiliary equipment, such as photocom-posing and developing machines, to produce *hard copy* (words printed on paper) of text material. He or she measures lines of copy and size of type to be input to determine machine settings required, using a printer's rule. The operator then loads a disc or tape into the machine and activates the keys to input copy while scanning a video screen to monitor the input, correcting errors as they occur. The operator then loads tape into a photocopying machine, setting the font selector control to select the size and style of type. The machine automatically prints text from the disc or tape on sensitized paper. The operator transfers the magazine of exposed paper to the developing machine, which develops the image of the text. The operator then corrects any errors on the tape, using the typesetting machine and video screen. Salary is usually $13 an hour or more.

Photocomposing Machine Operator

Photocomposing typesetting machines are found in the editorial production areas of newspapers and other publishing houses, away from the noise and dirt of the pressroom. This production worker sets up and operates the photocomposing machine to transfer letters and words from perforated or magnetic tape into black-and-white print on film or photographic paper. She or he loads a roll of photographic paper or film into the machine's magazine. The operator then places the roll of perforated tape on the machine reel and threads it through the feeder mechanism.

He or she chooses a type font and size and positions it on the photographic unit. It is adjusted for light intensity and then started. The machine automatically exposes type on film or paper, actuated by the coded signals on the perforated or magnetic tape. The machine may be equipped with computer interfacing that would control size and style of type, width of lines, hyphenating, and length of copy column. The operator removes and stacks the finished copy. He or she is responsible for performing user maintenance. Salary is usually $12 an hour or more.

Phototypesetting Equipment Monitor

These production workers monitor and control computer systems used in phototypesetting. They set control switches on optical character readers, computers, or typesetters. They receive and insert command codes to integrate and operate the equipment according to specific requirements contained in markup instructions from the designer of the piece. They select and load input and output units with material for operating the equipment. They operate switches to clear the systems and start operations. The operators observe the equipment during operation, looking for error lights, messages and machine stoppages, or faulty operation. They perform only the most basic user maintenance, such as cleaning the exterior. Salary is usually $12 an hour or more.

Word Processor

A term that refers to both the machines and their operators, *word processors,* are found at many modern newspapers, book and magazine printing houses, and publishers of every description. The operators receive copy and layout instructions and, using their knowledge of typesetting and typing, select the spacing on the keyboard of the machine. They adjust margins and other spacing mechanisms to set the line justification. They then type from marked copy, using an electric typewriter that simultaneously produces a proof copy (called a *strike on*) and a master tape. They make corrections by strikeover on proof copy, automatically making the identical correction on the master tape. In some cases, they retype the corrected portion only, generating a correction tape that is spliced into the master tape. They then install the master tape into a composer-output printer. The operators insert coated paper into a composer and operate the composer in response to function light indicators, changing type fonts and format as the work progresses. In many plants, the keyboard function is performed by other personnel at various terminals throughout the plant, and the operator alone runs the composer as master tapes are generated.

Word processors, especially those with experience in object pasting, earn in excess of $14 an hour or more, depending on location.

Keypunch Operator

Many firms of all descriptions employ a keypunch operator to transcribe data from source materials to punchcards, paper or magnetic tape, and magnetic cards, to record accounting or statistical data for subsequent printing. The operator attaches a skip bar to the machine and a previously punched program card around the machine drum to control duplication and spacing of constant data. The worker loads the machine with decks of tabulating punchcards, paper or magnetic tape, or magnetic cards.

He or she moves switches and depresses keys to select automatic or manual duplication and spacing, select alphabetic or numeric punching, and transfer cards or tape through the machine stations. The operator depresses keys to transcribe new data in prescribed sequence from source material into perforations on cards or as magnetic impulses on specified locations on tape or cards. Salary is usually $8 or more an hour.

Photolettering Machine Operator

This machine and its operator may be found in any establishment concerned with the creation of art for printing. A photolettering machine creates display type and headlines on film or photosensitive paper. The operator secures a roll of stock in the machine magazine and inserts specified film fonts in the machine reel. By turning the reel to specified selector marks, he or she positions the letters to be printed and moves a lever to expose the specified letter on film or paper. The operator pushes a cutter button to separate the strip of headline from the supply roll. The worker removes foreign material from rollers to prevent irregular imaging and may be required to clean and refill the tank of developing solution. An operator may be designated to this position as an added duty. Salary is usually $9 an hour or more.

POSITIONS IN HOT METAL TYPECASTING

Hot metal typecasting machines automatically assemble individual characters or lines of type.

Hot, molten metal is poured into the assembled type *matrices* (molds) and, when it cools and hardens almost instantaneously, lines of type are produced for letterpress printing or for making reproduction proofs for lithographic and other printing processes.

Positions in this field are generally found in small newspaper printing plants and a few remaining trade typesetting establishments. Job descriptions in hot metal typesetting are not included in this book because hot metal typecasting is a declining technology in the United States and the opportunities it offers are quite limited. Indeed, the *Occupational Outlook Handbook* of 1996 refers to hot-type text composition as "nearly extinct."

POSITIONS FOR COMMERCIAL ARTISTS

The graphic arts industry provides many opportunities for artists of every description. Every newspaper, for example, has an advertising design department. Most commercial printers employ one or more artists to design, illustrate, and paste up direct mail advertising, letterheads, newsletters, and other printed matter. Every printed piece must first be visualized. After the visual is approved, other artists may be used to prepare a mechanical from which a plate is made. The following positions are involved in the entire process, from visualization to final rendering.

Layout Artist

Many commercial, book, and magazine printers employ a creative graphic design artist to combine art and copy in a pleasing, easy-to-read, and compelling composition. The artist may design the printer's own promotional material or may design advertising material for customers.

She or he studies illustrations and photographs to plan the presentation of the product or service, designing the headline for maximum impact. The artist selects the size and style of type to be used, based upon the available space, knowledge of layout principles, and esthetic design concepts. Then he or she makes a rough sketch of the piece and presents it for interim approval. The artist may then prepare a comprehensive layout that is as close to the finished printed page as can be made. The layout artist prepares notes and instructions for the pasteup artist, who will assemble the elements of the printed page ready for the printer's camera. Salary may vary from $15,000 to $35,000 annually.

Package Designer

Commercial and package printers may employ package designers to create graphic designs or entire packages. The designers receive assignments from the customer or an art director, studying traditional, period, and contemporary design styles and motifs to determine what concept will be most suitable to the product. They review marketing trends and preferences of ultimate customers. The designers create and modify some preliminary sketches, conferring with the customer or art director until a consensus is reached. They then prepare a comprehensive drawing of each face of a package and assemble the drawings into a model of the package. They specify type size and style, provide instructions for ink colors and paper, or indicate other material selections. The package designer may be responsible for engineering specs to insure that the package will stand up to rough handling. The usual salary is $18,000 to $45,000 annually.

Forms Designer

Business forms printers employ a forms designer to work with customers in developing forms such as invoices, purchase orders, production schedules, and similar paperwork. Using drafting instruments, the forms designer makes a preliminary sketch of the form and submits it to the customer for approval. He or she specifies type and art and prepares a pasteup for printing preparation. The designer may also be involved with formatting, interleaving, and other considerations based on the capabilities and limitations of the press equipment available. The usual salary is from $20,000 to $35,000 annually.

Pasteup Artist

Many larger commercial printers, all newspapers and magazine printers, and other printing establishments have an art department in which the pasteup artist works. Pasteup artists are responsible for translating the concepts of the layout artist into a form that can be photographed and plated. They produce a *mechanical,* which is an assembly of type and photographs or art pasted down on a sheet of illustration board. They use rubber cement or melted wax coated on the back of the art elements to affix the elements to the board. In some applications, they work with a video screen, calling type and art elements from a computer memory and positioning them with an electronic "pencil" into a completed page. They prepare overlays for multicolor work and cut and peel away Rubylith or similar materials to create masks that will serve as clear windows marking the location of halftone illustrations. Pasteup artists may be called on to sketch simple line drawings, borders, and other adornments for the final printed piece. These craftspeople may earn $10 or more an hour.

Photograph Retoucher

This airbrush artist may be found in some printing plants, particularly newspapers, or may operate and own an independent studio. The retoucher sharpens and intensifies photographs, painting out unwanted details such as telephone poles and wires or other distracting elements. He or she also restores damaged or faded photos or colors or shades drawings to simulate a photograph, using the airbrush technique. The retoucher examines photos to determine the changes required and cuts out a masking template, using shears or a sharp knife blade, removing the mask from areas to be spray painted. Then she or he sprays color (or gray paint for black-and-white photos) over the area to be corrected, to change or alter perspective, color, or tone. The retoucher also builds up or tones down background areas to add contrast to the photo, restores details where required and adds highlights to improve texture. Some retouchers may specialize in product photograph retouching. Fifteen dollars or more an hour is the usual salary.

Engrosser/Calligrapher

This specialized artist may be found in printing plants specializing in diplomas, award certificates, and other document printing. He or she letters key words directly on the document by hand, using pen and ink. This craftsperson may be required to design and cut script and display type for reproduction. He or she may design and render floral and other adornments for book covers. Designing and rendering borders, scrollwork, and initial letters (swash initials) for books and magazines may also be required. Salary may be $20 an hour or more.

Letterer

These commercial artists may be employed in printing plants of all descriptions as well as in independent art studios. They paint or draw precise lettering of a style not normally found in type books.

Their work is employed in the headlines of printed advertisements or editorial material in books and magazines. Hand lettering is preferred over type because it can be tailored specifically to the space and subject matter of the article or advertisement it titles. These artists use lettering pens and brushes, working with ink or paint. They may be required to design lettering in an original face. The usual salary is $12 an hour or more.

OTHER POSITIONS IN PRE-PRESS OPERATIONS

Lithographic Platemaker and Grainer

All lithographic printing plants either employ a lithographic platemaker or use the services of a trade shop. The platemaker transfers positive or negative images from a flat to metal plates to produce a lithographic printing plate. He or she positions the plate under an arc lamp in a vacuum frame and places the negative or positive film over it under a bright light to transfer the film image to the light-sensitive coating on the plate. The operator washes the exposed plate in water and applies lacquers, developing inks, desensitizing etches, gum solutions, and asphaltum to develop the image on the plate.

Today, many of these operations are performed automatically. Salary ranges are as follows: black-and-white, $11 an hour; process color, $13 an hour or more.

Lithographic Stripper

This skilled craftworker is a vital link in the process of transferring type and pictures from originals to the printed page. He or she is employed in nearly all kinds of printing plants, including letterpress and gravure, where the worker may be called simply a stripper. The lithographic stripper positions negative (or positive) films on a layout sheet of goldenrod paper which, when it is completed, is called a flat. He or she works on an illuminated tabletop, using drafting tools and artists' work aids, such as a triangle, divider, straightedge, and magnifier. The stripper trims and fits negatives together and secures negatives to the goldenrod, using tape. Then he or she touches up the negative to opaque pinholes and other imperfections. Ruled lines and borders are drawn where required, using a scribing tool. Then the stripper inverts the flat on the table and cuts away the goldenrod behind the negatives to make an exposure window. Finally, he or she routes the completed flat to the platemaking department for further processing. If the job is to be printed in color, the stripper prepares a separate flat for each color. The usual salary range is $13 an hour or more.

Process Stripper

These specialized craftworkers are employed mostly by lithographic trade color separation shops. They evaluate and correct the color characteristics of four-color film negatives used in producing lithographic printing plates. They mount film negatives on

an illuminated viewer to determine the quality and color gradations, comparing a proof print of the negative with the customer's
sample illustration or standard color charts. They identify and
mark color discrepancies between the print and the color separation negative. They select tinted film strips or combine several to
achieve a specified color tone, trying them in turn until the correct
color is achieved. The craftworkers glue strips over sections of the
negative requiring correction and send negatives back to the camera for correction. They evaluate a proof print of the corrected
negative and route acceptable negatives to the production department for making into lithographic plates. Salary is usually $18 an
hour or more.

Lithographic Camera Operator

Most printing plants of any size have a graphic arts camera as
part of their basic equipment, including printing processes other
than lithographic printing. The camera operator uses a vertical or
horizontal camera to produce film or glass negatives and positives
used in the preparation of the printing plates. He or she mounts the
original art or photograph on the copy board and focuses the camera to enlarge or reduce the image. The operator selects and places
a screen at the focal plane to render shadings in black-and-white
dots. He or she also places color filters in position to isolate each
of the primary colors and black for full-color printing. The
craftsperson adjusts lights and exposes film for a specified length
of time, and then develops film in a series of chemical baths or
mounts unexposed film in a machine that automatically develops
and fixes the image. The same camera is used for photographing
pasted-up mechanicals. The usual salary is $13 an hour or more.

In some plants, a lithographic camera operator may also be
given the task of operating a step-and-repeat camera. This involves
the printing of one image repeated many times on a relatively large

sheet. He or she positions and aligns the copy in the camera holder and operates the camera, which automatically moves incrementally to expose a negative in measured steps.

Scanner Operator, Black-and-White and Color

Black-and-white scanners are found in many newspaper printing operations, while color scanners are used in the printing of magazines and direct-mail advertising. The scanner produces a screened film negative with a dot pattern that duplicates the tonal values of a continuous-tone photograph or piece of art. The color scanner scans for each of four colors used in full-color printing by means of a filter that screens out three of the colors on each pass. The scanner operator examines the copy to be reproduced for possible problems and plans the work to include corrections that may be programmed in the machine. The operator evaluates the intensity of color areas using a densitometer, sets the scanner dials for optimum results, and starts the machine, producing a positive or negative film for each of the primary colors and black, or a single negative or positive for black-and-white work. The usual salary is $12 an hour or more.

Laser Beam Color Scanner Operator

In many modern printing plants, the laser beam color scanner is replacing conventional scanners in producing sets of color separation negatives. The operator sets up the computer-controlled machine to enlarge or reduce and screen film separations used in the printing preparation of lithographic printing plates. He or she measures the original color transparency or color reflective copy to determine the square area of film required. Then the operator selects and cleans the specified scanner drum and head to insure dust-free processing and mounts the scanner drum and head on the scanner. He or she positions copy on the scanning drum and analyzes the original copy to evaluate color density, gradation highlights, middle tones, and shadows. Then the control knob of the computer is turned to obtain the desired effects. The operator selects a preprogrammed computer tape, positions the tape in the electronic screening section of the computer, and activates the console keys to input control information. He or she then loads the film into the chamber for exposing and activates the automatic vacuum system mechanism that loads and secures the film on the drum. The operator pushes a button to activate the scanner, unloads the film holder at completion of the scanning cycle, and develops the exposed film. Scanner operators are among the highest paid of the pre-press professions, with unionized operators earning an hourly wage of about $22.

Hand Etcher, Rotogravure

These production workers are found in the pressroom of large rotogravure or similar printing plants. They etch images on the surface of printing rollers that have been coated with photo or acid resist on which the image has been transferred photographically, using their knowledge of colors and etching and printing techniques. They study layout to determine etching requirements based on the color and the printing sequence. They lift the printing roller onto the brackets of the rinsing vat and tape the ends of the roller with masking tape to limit the etching to a specified width. The workers then rinse the roller to remove the coating from non-printing areas. They transfer the roller to an acid bath, turn a valve to agitate acid solution with compressed air, and start the machine to rotate the roller in the solution. Periodically the etchers remove the roller from the acid bath to inspect the depth of the etch. They scratch charcoal into the etched cavities to intensify the image for evaluation and transfer the roller to a rinsing vat to remove all the acid-resistant coating. The usual salary is $16 an hour or more.

Screen Maker, Hand and Photographic Process

Screen makers are employed by screen printing firms in the production of billboards, point-of-purchase displays, and textiles. They prepare stencils, using photographic equipment or cutting them by hand as required. They immerse gelatin coated pigment paper in a photosensitive solution and then press the gelatin side of the paper onto a transparent plate, using a squeegee. They position the photographic negative over pigment paper and expose negative, paper, and plate to bright light to develop a silk screen pattern on the plate. Then they strip negative and pigment paper from the plate and wash the plate to remove unexposed gelatin. They position the plate over silk screen material and press the plate, using a hand roller to transfer a gelatin pattern to the material. The workers fit and align a prefabricated frame over the silk screen, pour paint onto the screen, and force the paint through the pattern in the screen to make a sample print, using a squeegee. Salary is $16 an hour or more.

Photoengraver Retoucher

This production worker is normally found in a trade engraving shop or in large newspaper printers. The retoucher makes alterations to improve photoengraving film reproductions of sketches or photographs or to eliminate defects and distortions in design. He or she compares film negatives or positives with the original photo or art to locate portions of the images, such as dots and lines, that were lost during processing. The retoucher also looks for spots on the film or excessively dark or light tones. He or she paints in additional lines or dots with opaque ink to increase the intensity of the image on the film, or scratches out lines or dots to reduce the intensity, following the colors on the original to restore specific tone values. The retoucher may sketch designs on transparent paper before transferring them to film. The usual pay scale is $18 an hour or more.

Photostat Machine Operator

The photostat machine, used for making glossy or matte finish reductions or enlargements of original copy, may be found in some printing establishments but is more likely to be found in independent trade shops and art studios. The operator places a roll of sensitized paper in the machine, measuring length and width of material to be copied. Then he or she computes the percentage of enlargement or reduction necessary, using a percentage scale. The operator mounts original material on an easel beneath the lens, turns on light, moves controls to focus the lens on the material and estimates exposure time. He or she places the filter over the lens when making black-and-white prints from color originals. Exposed film is rolled inside the machine into a developer tank. The film is cut and cranked into a tray of fixing fluid attached to the machine. Then the operator examines the print for sharpness of line and places it in a heated dryer. The usual pay scale is $9 an hour or more.

Salary Differentials

You undoubtedly have noticed the significant variance in wages within each specialty. This is owing to a number of factors, including the location and size of the printing plants, the experience level of the operators and technicians, and the overall paucity of reliable national statistics. Many of the printing and related specialties organizations listed in Appendix B are compiling better data, which should help future printing professionals in their career decision-making. One thing, however, is clear. As the demands for more sophisticated technicians, computer operators, and savvy financial analysts grow, salaries will increase in order to attract talented and creative professionals to the industry.

CHAPTER 5

JOBS IN THE PRESSROOM AND BINDERY

PRESSROOM JOBS

The jobs described in this section are all located in or near the pressroom. Pressroom employees contribute their efforts to one main purpose: keeping the presses rolling. While the jobs are listed individually, many pressroom jobs are part of a team effort, especially those directly involved with the operation of the press.

Pressroom jobs, more than other jobs in printing, are filled under an apprenticeship program under union sponsorship. If you are seeking a career in the pressroom, emphasize your mechanical abilities and your ability to take that extra measure of care in your work.

You may find unfamiliar words in some of the job descriptions that follow. The glossary in Appendix E defines many printing terms.

Pressroom Supervisor

This middle-level manager supervises and coordinates the activities of workers engaged in making ready, operating, and feeding all the various types of presses found in the pressrooms of all printing establishments, such as newspapers, book printers, commercial printers, business forms printers, and others. He or she regularly observes the operation of presses and examines the output from the discharge stack of each operating press. The supervisor critically examines full-color work for dot registration and color fidelity. He or she coordinates the flow of work into the pressroom, ascertaining requirements in advance in order to plan day-to-day operations. The manager exercises the appropriate management skills in relationships with people above and below this level in the organization. When employed in an in-plant shop, this manager is called the Supervisor, Printing Department. The usual salary range is $22,000 to $50,000 annually.

Assistant Press Operator

These production workers may be found in any type of printing establishment, assisting the press operators of a lithographic, web, letterpress, flexographic, rotogravure, or business forms press. Some of their duties include, but are not limited to: make-ready, feeding, adjusting side guides and tension, monitoring ink fountain operation and roller distribution of ink, adjusting suction grippers, stocking supplies, removing printed sheets, and performing such other duties as the press operator may direct. One of the main functions is to keep the press clean and lubricated. Assistant press operators help with the monitoring of the press operation at run speed, reporting any faulty printing or press defects to the press operators. A usual pay scale is $10 an hour or more.

Rotogravure Press Operator

A rotogravure press prints by the gravure method with plates that are curved to fit around a cylinder. The rotogravure press operators make ready and operate the press. They install engraved copper plate(s) on the cylinder(s), adjusting *doctor,* or wiping, blades that remove excess ink from the surface of the plate at each cycling of the plate cylinder. They thread the web of paper through the feeder mechanism between the plate and impression cylinders, adjusting guides and tension bars. For multicolor printing, they set the focus of electronic scanners on the guidelines of the paper to automatically control color registration. If the press is so equipped, they regulate the temperature in the web drying chamber and adjust the automatic cutter at the discharge end of the press. Since a rotogravure press is usually very large, the press operators may direct the activities of a press crew, who may feed and unload the press, take care of ink levels in the fountains, clean the equipment, and perform other duties as the operator directs.

If the press is so equipped, the operators may be responsible for cutting, creasing, and folding, at the discharge end. The usual wage is $18 an hour or more.

Web Press Operator

A web press prints roll to sheet or roll to roll—meaning that the paper supplied to the press is fed from a roll and threaded through the impression and plate cylinders. The web press operator is a production worker who makes ready and oversees the operation of the press. Some web presses have more than one printing unit and may be capable of printing more than one roll of paper simultaneously. The press normally is used to print newspapers, books, periodicals, and business forms, generally in long runs that make it economical to use a large press requiring elaborate make-ready. The operator locks printing plates on curved cylinders and threads the forward edge of the paper web through the various cylinders, guides, and tension bars, inching the web through the press while adjusting feed controls. When plates become worn, the operator replaces them with make-over plates, performing the switch as quickly as possible to minimize downtime. If the web breaks, the press stops automatically and the operator must readjust tension bars.

Then the operator must activate a pasting device to join the ends of the web. The operator inspects finished *signatures* (groups of printed pages) for signs of faulty printing or press failures. The operator may be responsible for training apprentices and for user and higher maintenance levels. The usual pay scale is $18 an hour or more.

Engraving Press Operator

Die-stamping presses usually are found in greeting card and social stationery printing establishments. The operators of die-stamping presses make ready and operate the presses in the production of announcements, greeting and business cards, letterheads, and related items. They use wrenches to install appropriate die and inking rollers on the *ram* (plunger of the press). They cut out and fasten a paper template to the bed of the press to maintain the flatness of finished cards or sheets. They insert and adjust a roll of wiping paper that automatically cleans the die between impressions. They thin the ink to desired consistency and fill the ink fountains. They start the press to obtain proof copy, examine the proof, and adjust the press and ink fountain to obtain uniform coverage and indentation. They start the press and hand-feed cards or sheets as the press cycles at governed speed. They may be required to perform user maintenance. Wage is typically at $15 an hour or more.

Embossing Press Operator

Embossing presses are used in die-stamping shops for producing greeting cards, business cards, and stationery. Embossing press operators install and lock an embossed plate in the press's *chase* (frame), locking the chase in the bed of the press. They mix an embossing composition to a puttylike consistency, spread glue on the platen, and apply a thin pad of composition over the glue. They then make an impression of the embossing plate in the composition, trim off excess, and allow the composition to harden. They scrape the high spots on the composition to prevent it from puncturing the paper. They start the press, set sheets singly between guide pins, and emboss them, removing and stacking them as they are embossed. The usual wage is $10 an hour or more.

Metal-Decorating Lithographic Printing Press Operator

A metal-decorating press may be found in a container printing and packaging establishment, where descriptive matter and art are printed on flat sheets of tin, aluminum, or other metal before being formed into containers. The press operators set up and make ready, install lithographic plates on the press cylinders, and adjust feed guides, back and side gauges, and ink and dampening rollers. They mix ink colors according to specs and fill the ink fountain. They start the press and make a trial run, adjusting for color intensity, register, and fit. During the run, they observe the press and product, adjusting as necessary. They observe heat gauges and regulate heat intensity to achieve uniform drying. Where necessary, they perform user maintenance. The usual wage is $12 an hour or more.

Plastic Printing Press Operator

These production workers are found in flexographic printing plants, printing colored designs and copy on rolls of plastic film or plastic-coated materials. They position and clamp plates on the press, using hand tools. They pour ink into ink pans and thread plastic material through the press rolls. They start the press, inching the plastic web through the press to adjust side guides and other controls. They manipulate rheostats to regulate speed and feed of press and temperature of the drying oven. They examine printed sheets or rolls coming off the press to detect defects such as wrinkles, smears, and uneven color distribution.

They may be required to perform user maintenance on the press. The typical wage is $12 an hour or more.

Cloth Printer or Screen Printing Machine Operator

Screen printing on textiles is done in highly specialized plants. The operator is a production worker who mounts screens in specified sequences on the machine. He or she pours printing paste onto screens or fills the automatic feed pan. The operator adjusts machine speed and swing and pressure of squeegees, depending on the type of cloth being printed and the design. The operator starts the machine and the conveyor belt that carries the textile under the screen(s). He or she also inspects cloth to detect faulty printing and inaccurate register. During the run, the operator inspects the product to insure that it meets quality standards and specs. The operator may be required to perform user maintenance. The usual wage is $12 an hour or more.

Offset Duplicating Machine Operator

Offset duplicating machines are found in almost any sizable establishment, whether or not it is engaged in printing. The operator installs a presensitized metal or paper plate on the plate cylinder of the machine and also checks ink and dampening levels and paper stock supplies. He or she turns the elevator crank to raise the feed table to the proper height and sets dial controls to adjust the speed and feed of the machine according to the weight of the paper. The machine automatically reproduces copy by the offset process. The operator cleans and files plates for possible later use and may operate an automatic platemaker.

The operator may perform user maintenance on the machines as required. The usual wage is $10 an hour or more.

Press Maintenance Person

In all but the very largest plants, maintenance is performed as an extra duty by the press operator, who adjusts and repairs offset litho presses and letterpresses, confining repairs to user echelon levels.

He or she also lubricates and cleans the presses, replacing worn or broken parts, and disassembles and cleans ink rollers, dampening rollers, and parts. The press maintenance person may be required to repair and adjust heat dryers. The usual hourly wage is $15 or more.

Slitter, Creaser, Scorer, Slotter Operator

These production workers may be found in package printing plants as part of the assembly line prior to the printing of corrugated or plain paperboard containers. One machine may do all or some of the operations of slitting, creasing, scoring, and slotting. The operators set and operate the machine, turning screws and moving picker feed bar and feed table guides to accommodate the appropriate sheet size. They position slitting, scoring, and creasing dies by sliding dieheads along a drive shaft over the machine bed to achieve the specified size blank.

They adjust to obtain specified depths and location of slots and creases. They may operate a machine that cuts off container blanks from rolls of corrugated or plain paperboard. They also verify dimensions of blanks by measurement and observe the performance of a machine to detect malfunctions. The usual salary is $10 an hour or more.

Tag Press Operator

This production worker is employed in tag and label printing and manufacturing establishments. He or she sets up and operates a machine that prints, cuts, and punches holes in paperboard to form paper tags and labels.

The operator reads the work order to determine the type of setup required. He or she mounts paperboard rolls on a machine dispensing spindles, using a jack or hoist, and installs and adjusts printing plates into the bed of the press. The operator mounts rolls of reinforcing paperboard onto the machine, threading the ends through the stamping section and filling the machine with metal grommets where required. The worker spreads a specified color of ink in the ink reservoir, adjusts the angle of the cutting blade, using an allen wrench, and turns valves to adjust the timing of the cutting blade and the punch. Then the operator starts the machine and observes performance to detect malfunctions.

He or she removes completed tags or labels from the discharge end, stacks the products into boxes in specified amounts, and stacks the boxes on skids. The usual pay scale is $10 an hour or more.

Carbon Paper Interleafer

This production worker in the business forms printing plant tends a machine that brings together webs of carbon paper and paper stock fed from rolls. The machine then winds the combined webs onto a single roll of specified length. The operator exercises care to prevent wrinkling of the stock as it passes through the machine. She or he installs the appropriate rolls of stock on dispensing spindles using a hoist.

The operator adjusts the paper guides and tension controls, reads a counter that records the footage, and stops the machine when the proper footage has been achieved. He or she also performs user-level maintenance on the machine as required. The pay scale is $9 an hour or more. This position is being phased out of some plants as businesses decrease their use of carbon in favor of newer, carbonless paper.

Quick Print Printer

This production worker/manager may also be found in smaller captive shops called *in-plant printers.* He or she sets up and operates printing presses, generally of the duplicator type, as well as automatic platemakers, paper-cutting, drilling, and folding machines. The printer duplicates negatives on photosensitive metal plates, using exposure frame. He or she develops an image on the plate and washes the plate to make it ready for the press. The craftsperson sets metal type in a *chase* (frame) by hand, where required. He or she mounts the litho plate on the cylinder of the press and may also mount type on the cylinder or bed of a cylinder press. This worker/ manager orders paper stock and materials, including chemicals and ink, and may have to discuss printing requirements with customers. He or she keeps records of time and materials for billing. The quick-print printer may be required to maintain and repair shop equipment. The pay scale is $9 an hour or more.

Plate Setter, Flexography

These production workers would be found in many flexographic printing establishments, most of which are engaged in package printing. Plate setters prepare cylinders for installation in the press by measuring and cutting brass plates of specified dimensions. They bend the plate to the curvature of the cylinder using a plate-curving machine. They lift and place a printing cylinder of the specified size on a proof machine holding rack. They measure and draw centering lines on the cylinder to be used as guides for alignment of plate and dies. Then they slide the formed plate on a cylinder, position the plate according to centering lines, and clamp the plate in place with tension bands.

They use a knife to trim and bevel rough edges of rubber dies. They position dies on the cylinder plate, following guide markings and diagrams, and fasten dies to the plate with adhesive paper. Then they apply ink to the dies with a roller and operate a proof machine to make a trial impression on proof paper. They correct errors on the original setup until the trial impression meets quality standards. The usual pay scale is $10 an hour or more.

Bag Machine Operator

This production worker tends a machine that automatically measures, prints, cuts, folds, and glues (or seals) plain or wax papers, polyethylene film, or other plastic films to form bags. The operator threads material from the parent roll through guides and rollers to cutters, gluer (or electric heat-sealer device), printer, and folder. He or she starts the machine as slow speed, observes the operation to detect a malfunction or faulty feeding or printing, and adjusts the machine to achieve uniformity and conformance with specs. The operator may be responsible for handling the parent rolls of bag material, using jacks and a hoist. The operator also performs user-level maintenance of the machine as required. The wage scale is $10 an hour or more.

Bag Printer

Bag printing is done in specialized printing establishments that may or may not be part of a package printing and converting operation.

It consists of printing data and designs such as brand name, trademark, contents description and/or analysis, and other data on paper or textile sacks. The operator inserts specified type or plates into slots in the plate cylinder, locking the plates in place. He or she pours appropriate color ink into the ink fountain and positions a supply of sacks on the press feed bed. The operator then starts the press and activates the rotary drum and feed mechanism and feeds individual sacks into the press. He or she then removes the printed bags and stacks them for further processing. The operator also cleans the press and performs user maintenance. The wage scale is $10 an hour or more.

Envelope Converter/Printer Operator

Many envelope converters also print corner cards on envelope die-cut blanks or paper rolls. These production workers set up, adjust, and maintain a battery of automatic machines that make and print the envelopes.

They install gears, plungers, and rollers onto the machine and turn set screws to adjust feeding, folding, gumming, and sealing, and apply glassine to window envelopes as necessary. They operate the machine for a trial run, measuring the dimensions of the first piece off with a rule to confirm that it meets specifications. During the run, they observe the performance of the machine and the products to detect malfunctions. These operators are capable of disassembling the machine to repair or replace worn or broken parts. They perform user level of maintenance as required. Salary is $10 or more an hour.

Decorating Printer, Glass

Glass decorating is done by the silk screen method, usually in container plants. It is capable of high-quality, full-color printing, although in most applications quality printing is not a requirement. This production worker sets up manually controlled or automatic decorating equipment.

He or she bolts chucks to the conveyor of the automatic equipment to accommodate containers of specified sizes. The worker adjusts the feeder mechanism to adjust the stroke of the machine so that the design will be placed in the proper location on the container. Then he or she adjusts the squeegee blade so that the proper amount of ink is deposited on the surface of the container. The worker performs user maintenance on decorating equipment as required. The pay scale is $12 an hour or more.

Box Printer

Box printing is done in specialized plants that may be associated with packaging operations. The box printer sets up and operates the machine to print trademarks, designs, or identifying information on cardboard boxes and sleeves, or sometimes on wooden boxes. He or she fastens type or plate to a holding mechanism in the press. Boxes may be loaded into feed hoppers, which automatically position the box on a conveyor belt passing under the printing head. In other applications, the operator may place the boxes one at a time under the printing head, depressing a foot pedal to activate printing. In either case, she or he is responsible for uniform ink coverage and even impressions of the image. The operator performs user maintenance as required. The pay is usually $10 or more an hour.

BINDERY JOBS

A multitude of jobs exist in the binding or finishing end of the printing industry, only some of which are described here because of space limitations. The actual printing of a product such as a book or magazine is only one step in its production. Cutting, creasing, folding, gathering, and stitching are all just as vital to the completion of the job.

A bindery worker must be especially careful to avoid mistakes because the substrates he or she handles have already had value added in the form of labor and materials. A mistake at this stage of the process can mean that all the labor invested in the product up to this point must be scrapped at great cost to the firm. Bindery workers should have good mechanical ability as well as good attention to detail.

Bindery Supervisor

This middle-level manager supervises binderies, which may be located within large commercial printers or periodical and book printers or may exist as separate trade shops. The supervisor coordinates the activities of workers engaged in forming, finishing, and covering books, magazines, and catalogs. He or she reviews work orders to plan work goals and coordinates the receiving of signatures, paper stock, and other materials required to complete the job. This worker exercises the managerial skills required in any industry to maximize a group effort. He or she may only be required to supervise workers engaged in forming operations such as folding, cutting, gathering, and stitching or sewing, but often the person also is responsible for the training of new workers and for overall maintenance of bindery equipment. The salary range is $15,000 to $50,000 annually.

Bindery Worker

Machines that do corner cutting, embossing, scoring, stitching, taping, gluing, punching, and index tab attaching are found in most commercial printing plants. The production worker responsible for these operations may tend one or more machines. He or she positions stock against machine guides, starts the machine, and depresses a pedal to actuate production.

The worker observes the machine during the production run to maintain dimensions against specs. He or she may perform user-level maintenance as required. The pay scale is $9 an hour or more.

Casing-in-Line Setter

These bindery production workers perform duties in a bookbinding shop. They set up machines that automatically perform in sequence such operations as rounding and backing, *supering* (applying strip of reinforcing material to back of book), lining, casing-in, and pressing to convert gathered signatures into a finished book. They mount rolls of cloth and paper lining and headbands on machine spindles. They fill the glue pot and adjust the flow of glue. Then they adjust guides, holding clamps, rollers, rounding forms, and other machine parts to accommodate specified-size books. They turn the handwheel to position the press head according to the thickness of the book and the amount of pressure to be applied. Then the cutting mechanism is adjusted to cut linings and headbands to book size. The workers start the machine to produce a sample book and verify the accuracy of the setup before proceeding. They perform user maintenance on component parts as required. The pay scale is $10 an hour or more.

Gathering Machine Setter

This production worker is employed in a bookbinding shop where he or she sets up and operates a machine that gathers signatures for binding into books and magazines. The worker adjusts the machine pockets to accommodate the appropriate size signatures. He or she manipulates the dials to required graduations to set grippers and gripper feelers according to the thickness of the signatures being gathered. Then the worker installs and adjusts a jogging tray at the end of the line to true up the edges of the gathered signatures for trimming. He or she may be required to perform user maintenance on the gathering machine as required. The pay scale is $10 an hour or more.

Book Trimmer

This bookbindery production worker must have good powers of concentration and superior attention to detail. He or she tends a paper-cutting machine that cuts the edges of unbound books, magazines, and catalogs after they come off the press and prior to binding. The trimmer positions sections (or signatures) against the guide to trim the top, bottom, and front edges of the book to specified dimensions. Starting the machine, the stack of signatures are jogged against the paper guide(s) to achieve a true edge. Top, bottom, and front edges are trimmed in turn, activated by a treadle or a pair of levers protected with a safety device. The pay rate is $9 an hour or more.

Bookbinder

This skilled craftsperson is found in book printing shops and in independent trade shops engaged in manufacturing books of all descriptions. He or she cuts, sews, and glues components to bind books, using sewing machine, hand press, and hand cutter. The bookbinder may fold sheets into signatures or receive them from the press already formed into signatures, gathering them into numerical order. He or she operates a machine that sews signatures together to form a book body. The craftsperson compresses sewed signatures to conform to specified book thickness using a hand press or smashing machine. Then he or she trims the edges of the book to size and inserts the book body in a device that forms the back edge of the book into a convex shape. Glue is applied to the back of the book body and a cloth backing and headband are attached.

The worker applies color to the edges of signatures where called for, using brush, pad, or atomizer. Then he or she cuts the binder board to a specified size, cuts cover material to a specified size, and fits and glues the material to a binder board. Then the worker places glue outside the end papers of the book body to cover the board. Bound books are placed in a press that exerts pressure on the cover until the glue dries. The bookbinder may imprint the cover with gold lettering or designs, using a stamping machine. Some or all of the above operations may be performed automatically on specialized machines. The salary usually is $12 or more an hour.

Book Jacket Machine Operator

Due to the complexity of the machine, the operator needs better-than-average setup skills. The machine combines paper and plastic film to make jacket covers for books. The operator mounts rolls of paper and plastic film on a dispensing mechanism, using mechanical hoists. He or she installs rolls of adhesive tape on either side of the machine, used to splice the ends of new rolls to the previous ones. The operator then fills the flue reservoir and makes machine alterations to fulfill size specs. Then the machine is started and gradually brought up to speed while ensuring that the covers maintain the proper dimensions. The operator observes for proper gluing operation as the machine operates, cuts covers to size, and tapes edges. The operator replenishes the stock, clears jams, and performs user-level maintenance as required. The pay typically is $10 or more an hour.

Perfect Binder Setter

Perfect binding may be done in a book or magazine printing establishment, in a large commercial printer, or in a separate trade binding shop. The machine setters set up the multi-operation book-binding machine according to job specifications. The machine, or machines working in tandem, automatically gathers, compresses, stitches, or glues signatures into book or magazine bodies, then glues covers to form paperbound books and magazines. Operators install feed guides, holding clamps, pockets, rollers, and other machine parts to accommodate the book or magazine being assembled. They start up the machine to produce a sample for checking. They may be required to perform user maintenance. The pay scale is usually $10 or more an hour.

Folding Machine Feeder

Nearly every printing plant operates a folding machine of some description. Some folders have the capability of making only one or two parallel folds, others can make a series of parallel and right-angle folds. These production workers tend a machine that folds paper booklets, pamphlets, book and magazine signatures, and other printed matter. The operators turn a series of hand-wheels to adjust the folding slot opening and adjust the backstop according to a sample, using a rule and wrench. They start the machine and move a lever to engage a clutch that activates the folding blade and discharge conveyor rolls. They feed printed items against the backstop of the machine, synchronizing feeding with the action of the folding blade. Then they remove folded items from the discharge table and tack them on pallets for further processing. They may rub the folded edge with a wooden doctor blade to crease it. They also may hand-fold sheets when the capability of the machine is exceeded. The usual pay rate is $12 an hour.

Guillotine Operator

These production workers exercise great care and accuracy in the operation of a paper cutter. They set up and operate the machine, which has a heavy blade similar to the guillotine from which it derives its name. The machine cuts paper stock in stacks preparatory to binding; it also cuts paper in the proper size for delivery to the printing press. The operators review the sequence of cuts, measuring from the edge of the paper with the scale installed on the cutter, then set guides, clamps, and knives to cut paper to the exact size required. After placing the stack of paper on the bed of the machine, they fan the edges to allow the individual sheets to align themselves against the paper glue, using the hand or a stick to ensure a true edge. Using both hands as a safety measure, they pull levers simultaneously on either side of the cutter to activate the blade. They then remove the stack of paper and place it on a skid alongside for delivery to the press or the bindery. They are responsible for lubricating and clearing the cutter. The pay scale is $10 or more an hour.

Collating Machine Operator

This business forms bindery machine may stand alone or may be interfaced with a business forms press. The collator operator tends the machine or add-on component that assembles, perforates, glues, folds, and cuts multicopy business forms and carbon inserts into sets. He or she sets an indexing control to numbered positions corresponding to the number of sheets to be assembled. Then the operator fills the flue reservoir and feeds sheets reverse order (last sheet first) into a machine that integrates sheets, glues top edges, and cuts sheets into sets. Completed sets are stacked in bundles of a specified number. The operator places tolls of paper and carbon paper on feed spindles, using a hoist. He or she may punch holes in a completed set using a drill punch. The operator may be required to perform user maintenance. The usual pay rate is $13 an hour.

CHAPTER 6

THE JOB SEARCH

If you leave this chapter with nothing else fixed in your mind, let it be this: All your job-hunting efforts should be focused on one overriding objective—*to project a favorable image of yourself during the job interview.* All the other steps in your job-hunting campaign should lead to that one objective.

PRE-INTERVIEW STEPS

Let's describe the steps leading to the interview:

1. Make an assessment of your skills, strengths, and weaknesses—be honest.
2. Choose the field you wish to work in—the intermediate job and the ultimate goal.
3. Write a resume in which you outline your work and/or school experience, the job you are seeking, and your goal.
4. Write a cover letter.
5. Develop a prospect list, including telephone numbers.
6. Develop a references and testimonial file.
7. Practice the interview. This should take up about half of all your preliminary job hunting.

Having done these things, analyze your present situation. Unless it is desperate, don't be in any hurry to land a job, any job. You want the best job you can get, given your qualifications. Don't settle for anything less, because you may find yourself trapped in a job you dislike with dim prospects for the future, and there can be nothing worse in life than that.

Don't settle for "security," either. In today's dynamic economy, few jobs can offer real security, so don't place too much weight on supposed security in deciding which jobs to go after.

After analyzing your situation, you can determine how much time you can afford to spend in your job search. Then you can go about planning an organized step-by-step effort with one all important goal: a favorable interview.

A PERSONAL VIEWPOINT

In the course of 50 years in the printing and publishing business, the author of this book has interviewed as many as a thousand job seekers, of which a third were hired. And those applicants who were invited for an interview were only a fraction of those who responded to our help-wanted ads and other job search efforts.

Why were some applicants not invited for an interview, and why were some who were interviewed not hired? The answers to these questions will help you in your own job hunting. If you know why someone else has failed, it will help you to avoid the same pitfalls. This is known as learning the easy way. It is infinitely better than learning the hard way.

People of maturity and experience will tell you that all the important events in their lives and business careers had one thing in common. They started with a simple act—the act of sticking out a hand and saying, "Glad to meet you." All the important people in our lives—spouse, teacher, friend, employer—must first be met, one on one. Seen in this light, your first encounter with people is absolutely vital to your success or failure.

When you approach a first encounter with a new person in your life, an alarm should go off in your head. Since you don't know what the future will bring, and you have no idea how important that person may be in your future, you should be at your absolute best at every first meeting.

A successful real estate developer once said, "I will never be so wealthy that I can afford to have even one enemy." This might be paraphrased to apply to a job seeker: You will never be so successful that you can afford to make even one unfavorable first impression. Remember this one important fact: In every case, no employee of our firm was ever hired without making a favorable impression *during the interview.*

This does not mean that we have hired only people with striking personalities who could talk interestingly and convincingly. Far from it. Favorable impressions are created when the applicant is perceived as sincere, industrious, energetic, and competent. All other factors being favorable, these qualities will lead to a "Welcome aboard!"

ASSESSING YOUR SKILLS

In assessing your skills, don't neglect the less definable attributes—your strengths and weaknesses. Here is a list of discussion points that will help you to determine just how skillful you are. It may also help you to unearth some skills you possess but didn't know you had.

MANAGEMENT SKILLS

In working with others, do you tend to take over the project? Do you get the feeling that the project will fail unless the other team members do things differently? Do you feel a sense of responsibility for the success of the project? If you answer "yes" to these questions, you probably have at least a basic disposition toward being a supervisor. Try positions in which you can progress toward a supervisory role.

On the other hand, if you are content to be a member of the team, to do the job you are assigned to do without questioning it, then you can consider yourself a person who will perform best at a job where the work must be done without risk taking. Some of the most skillful members of the printing community are basically workers with little significant contact with other workers, such as typesetters, camera operators, and pasteup artists.

CREATIVITY

Are you generally dissatisfied with things as they are? When you encounter a procedure, a grouping of people or things, or any set of rules that have been followed by others in the past, do you have an urge to change them? Do you frequently have original ideas? If so, you should consider a career where creativity is required, such as any art career—layout artist, package designer, or letterer.

GENERAL KNOWLEDGE

Are you knowledgeable in such subjects as history, current events, language, and geography? Do you read to advance your knowledge as well as for pleasure? Do you read the editorial page of your newspaper as well as the general news? A person with good general knowledge is an asset in almost any job, mainly because it indicates good basic intelligence.

MATHEMATICAL ABILITY

Are you quick with figures? More importantly, do you *enjoy* working with figures? In printing, a good mathematical mind is a valuable quality, because so much of printing has to do with numbers: number of pages per signature, number of impressions per hour, cost per page, and so on. Mathematical ability is vital to a cost accountant or printing estimator. If you don't enjoy numbers, you may be better advised to seek employment in the creative side of printing or as a sales representative.

MECHANICAL ABILITY

Do you have a gift for fixing things? Do you try to figure out how a new machine or gadget works when you first see it? If you can answer "yes," you would be happy in the production end of the equipment-intensive printing industry. Printers must understand the capabilities and limitations of the machines they work with, and they should be capable of performing user maintenance. Some machines require the most delicate adjustments, such as the amount of ink or water to deliver to an offset press. A good sixth sense concerning machinery is useful here.

PRECISION PROFICIENCY

Are you a stickler for exactness? Are you happy with jobs that require working to very small tolerances? Do you try to avoid mistakes in any kind of situation? If so, the printing industry will welcome you. As you have read elsewhere in this book, a printer's mistake means doing the entire job over again, or living with it as long as it exists. Some jobs in printing that require a sense of the precise are lithographic stripper, pasteup artist, camera operator, and paper cutter operator, to mention a few.

PEOPLE ORIENTATION

Do you like meeting new people? Do you approach a meeting with pleasure, instead of shyness or dread? The person who is easy with others will make a good team member in the printing industry, as well as a good sales representative.

Many large firms require a team of several persons in their operation. A spirit of teamwork is essential to a successful and efficient operation. Of course, it goes without saying that a sales representative must enjoy relating to people.

AGGRESSIVENESS

Do you enjoy a competitive situation, either in sports or in everyday activities? Do you feel challenged by another's accomplishments? This aggressiveness translates into personal ambition, a quality that makes the person possessing it a valuable addition to any working staff. By always striving to be better individually, the person advances the achievements of the whole organization.

DEPENDABILITY

What has been your record of dependability over the years? Have you attained a good or better record of attendance at school or work? Do you finish a job you start out to do? The leader of any team or organization must depend on a predictable performance from each member of the team. A good prior record is an excellent indicator of a dependable team player.

THE PROFIT MOTIVE

Few people will ever admit to a desire for money in the course of the interview. You should assess this trait as thoroughly as your other good or bad points. The desire for money is not a weakness. In the marketplace, it is a definite asset. An honest admission that you desire good pay, as much as you can get, will probably earn more respect from the interviewer than skirting the issue.

Having culled all your assets from the previous pages, commit them to memory. They are as much a part of your selling points as your education and experience. Write a few sentences listing and explaining your assets. Examples: "I am dependable. In school, I was never absent and late only three times in four years." "I am very good with figures." "I had straight A's in algebra and geometry in high school. I am a stickler for perfection. Here's a little brochure I designed and printed." "That's good quality printing, don't you agree?"

You should memorize similar statements about your own attributes and be prepared to recite them during the interview, as easily as you would your social security number or telephone number. They are every bit as important.

CHOOSING YOUR OCCUPATION

You have made a complete assessment of your skills and abilities, and now you are ready to select the occupation, or at least the general field in the printing industry in which you want to work. You will base the selection on your assessment of your skills and abilities, though you should exercise caution in this respect. An important consideration, apart from your qualifications, is the potential the job offers you in terms of growth and personal gratification.

As we have said before, the fastest-growing segment in the printing industry is the pre-press phase. But a closer look at that growth reveals that much of it comes about because of new labor-saving machines and devices, particularly those in the high-technology electronic and computer-related fields. So, while pre-press operations are on the leading edge of the new printing technologies, it is possible that the job opportunities are more abundant in the other phases: administration, pressroom, and bindery operation.

The printing industry, like most industries in the computer age, is undergoing rapid change. The qualifications that fitted a person to a job five or ten years ago may now be obsolete, requiring additional new qualifications to perform the same task. For example, press operators on a conventional press in the past needed to rely on their judgment or experience. With today's highly automated presses, press operators instead must be capable of reading and understanding a control panel as complicated as that of an airliner. The seat-of-the-pants skill required a few years ago has been replaced by the seat of intelligence!

In choosing your occupation, you should select an intermediate job and an ultimate goal. If you plan to become a platemaker or stripper, your ultimate goal might be supervisor of the pre-press operation of a plant. Of course, bear in mind that careers do not always proceed in the orderly way you expect. But keep that ultimate goal in mind, and don't be timid about expressing it during the interview.

WRITING A RESUME

A resume is a bare-bones outline of your vital statistics, your education and training, your work experience, and your goals. It should be concise, informative, well organized, and easy to read. And since you will be seeking a job in the printing industry, it should be cleanly reproduced on good-quality paper. Here are some tips to bear in mind when you produce your own:

ORGANIZE THE RESUME

The following structure is recommended by most employment counselors.

1. Who you are: Name, address, home and work phone numbers and/or E-mail address.

2. What you are (or would like to be): Description or title of job you are seeking.

3. Work experience: List the jobs you have held, in chronological order, starting with the most recent. Don't neglect military service and part-time jobs, however remote the experience might seem from the work you are seeking. On each job, be sure to include the dates, name, and address of the employer, and name of supervisor. While most counselors recommend brevity in furnishing information on the resume, all are agreed that the duties in a previous job should be described fully.

4. Nonwork experience: Examples: Scouting, church volunteer, hobbies (only if they are in some way related to printing), and civic organizations. Duties, titles, and dates.

5. Special skills: Language proficiency, teacher or teacher assistant, sports or other competitive awards, or any other special skill or rating, such as pilot's license or first aid certificate.

6. Education: High school and/or college, degrees, certificates, majors and minors, any special training.

7. Summary: A statement about references being available upon request. You should include a statement about salary expectations and date of availability.

REWRITE FOR CLARITY

After writing the resume the first time, try rewriting it several times to get your sentences clear and complete. If grammar is not your strongest point, get someone to help with it. Then "boil it down" so that it occupies one page preferably, two at the most. But don't abbreviate. You are not composing a classified ad. Sample resumes are provided at the conclusion of this chapter.

WRITING A COVER LETTER

A cover letter should accompany each copy of your resume, whether you mail it or leave it with the interviewer. The purpose of the cover letter is to advertise the fact that you are job hunting, that you believe yourself to be qualified, and that you seek employment especially in the employer's firm. Cover letters must always be addressed specifically to a single firm or individual, *never* "To Whom It May Concern."

The cover letter should have all the features of any good advertising letter. Remember the acronym AIDA: *Attention, Interest, Desire,* and *Action.* In the first paragraph of the letter, you should capture the attention of the reader by a couple of sentences that promise a solution to a problem: "It is my pleasure to submit the enclosed resume in response to your advertisement in the city paper for a phototypesetter operator. I believe I have the qualifications necessary for the position."

You have captured the employer's attention because you are responding to the company's need for help. You promise a solution by expressing the belief that you are qualified.

In the second paragraph, you arouse the employer's interest by highlighting your main qualifications: "The position you advertise especially interests me because I excelled in the operation of the phototypesetter in my four years at Metro Tech. I believe I would enjoy the work, and especially working at Metro Press."

In the third paragraph, you elaborate on the points you made in the second paragraph, arousing the employer's desire to learn more: "My instructor at Metro Tech told me that I had a special aptitude for typesetting. I have always been an excellent speller and possess strong grammatical skills."

In the last paragraph, you pave the way for the employer to take action: "I would greatly appreciate a personal interview to discuss my qualifications further and to show you samples of my work. The interview can be scheduled at your convenience. May I call you early next week to make an appointment?" It is better to leave the initiative in your hands, although if the employer wants to see you sooner, your telephone number is on your resume.

Remember, the cover letter is a supplement to your resume: Don't repeat in the letter what is covered in the resume. Make your sentences short and to the point. Each paragraph should not exceed one or two sentences. The cover letter should not overwhelm the resume—plan it so it does not exceed a single typewritten page, with plenty of white space around it so that it is inviting to read.

DEVELOPING A PROSPECT LIST

Your job search will fall into three different categories: cold turkey, referrals, and classified ad responses. *Cold turkey* means you send your resume and a cover letter unsolicited to as many firms and individuals as possible. This also is known as "broadcasting" your resume. *Referrals* means following leads supplied by "friends of a friend." Responding to newspaper classified ads is routine, but don't forget that trade publications carry help wanted ads, too. The major U.S. trade magazines are provided in Appendix D.

Remember this important fact: you can't predict where, how, when, and with whom you will connect. Fully 60 to 70 percent of all jobs are not advertised at all, according to government statistics. The majority of jobs are filled from unsolicited inquiries from job seekers, or from referrals by business associates.

A prospect list is vital to your successful job search. It should contain as many names as you can muster, because you want the list to cover every possibility. The most obvious source for a prospect list is the "Printers" section in the phone book's yellow pages, but don't stop there. In addition to the Printers heading, there are other headings that are less well-known: Color Separators, Copying and Duplicating Services, Engraved Stationery, Lithographic Negatives and Plates, and many others.

Most yellow pages contain an index to make it easier for you to find the headings. Also, there are many printing installations in firms that are not primarily in the printing business. As an example, insurance companies often operate an in-house printing plant to produce insurance policies and other printed material. These captive shops are not listed as such in the Yellow Pages, but you may find that they are members of the local graphic arts professional association in your area. Most such associations maintain a job search exchange which could put you in contact with the in-house printers, although they probably would not permit you access to their membership list. The association normally screens job applicants and forwards promising resumes to interested members. The members then contact the applicant directly. Consult the list of local graphic arts associations given in Appendix C for the name and address of the one nearest you.

In developing a prospect list from among firms in the private sector, don't neglect the other sectors that also offer job opportunities: government, education, and nonprofit. To find federal, state, and municipal offices, look in the white pages of your telephone book.

Federal offices are listed under "U.S. Government," and state and municipal offices are listed under the name of the city and state. In most cases, you will not apply directly to the target printing plant, but to a central personnel office.

How many names? This is like asking how long a person's legs ought to be. In response to that question, Abraham Lincoln said they should be long enough to reach the ground. Your list should include every potential employer in your area. How can you be sure that you have all the names? For this you will have to turn to outside help: libraries, local chamber of commerce, and school job counselors.

Libraries have numerous directories and reference materials that might contain the information you seek. Seek out the librarian personally—he or she is usually knowledgeable and eager to be of assistance. Your local chamber of commerce will be glad to offer any assistance it can, which may even mean that it will make its membership list available to you. Job counselors in schools and colleges have access to a great deal of reference material, including books and pamphlets on how to land a job.

Develop a referral network. Along with the development of an actual list of prospects to whom you will broadcast your cover letter and resume, you also should develop a personal reference network. Simply stated, this means talking to people. It does not mean that you ask everyone you meet for a job. Your purpose in talking to others is twofold: to learn the identity of any person who might know someone in a printing plant, and to let it be known that you are looking for a job.

Consider this: everyone who is active in business knows at least 500 to a 1,000 individuals, most of them by name and occupation. If you "tap" this resource, by talking to a dozen people you may be sending out feelers to an untold number of connections, any one of which could result in that ultimate reward, the interview...and the job offer.

Once you have a name, you can contact that person for further information about the target employer, such as the name of the hiring executive, size and location of the plant, and kind of work. Now you have two names for your cover letter, which might begin thus: "Dear Mr. Smith: Ms. Helen Jones, who works in your bindery department, gave me your name. She said you are the person I should contact in my search for a position with your company...." The use of a name known to your prospect captures the reader's attention and sets the stage for your selling message.

To sum up your prospect list development: consult the yellow and white pages, seek help from your local graphic arts association and chamber of commerce, and talk to as many people as you can—librarians, job counselors, and the people you contact daily.

DEVELOPING A REFERENCE AND TESTIMONIAL FILE

There are two main types of references: personal and professional. Personal references are furnished by teachers, ministers, and influential friends. They concern such generalities as honesty, dependability, cheerfulness, and so on. Personal references usually are considered worthless by prospective employers, because no job applicant would submit an unfavorable evaluation. However, even though they have limited effect, your reference file should contain at least three or four such documents. If you're lucky enough to possess one from a *very* influential person, such as a member of Congress or a prominent citizen, by all means produce it during the interview.

Professional references are more to the point—they have to do with your performance on the job, and they are scrutinized carefully by the interviewer. They come from former academic teachers and/or instructors at your technical school, supervisors at your previous employment, and from coworkers, this last source not to be minimized..

Because of laws governing unemployment insurance, laws forbidding job discrimination, and other restrictions, many large corporation lawyers advise against furnishing references to departing employees, fearing that too-detailed references would make them liable to court action in the event of any future claims or charges. As a result, professional references are rare or, at best, so sketchy and generalized as to be ineffective. If you find yourself unable to obtain a reference from management, try going to a former coworker instead.

Here are some questions you might ask the coworker in outlining a professional reference:

- How long have you known me?
- What was the name of the firm we both worked for?
- What were my titles and duties?
- What was our relationship on the job?
- How would you evaluate my performance on the job?
- How was my record of attendance?
- Would you rehire me if you had the authority?

You should remind the coworker that he or she may be called by your prospective employer to confirm facts. You might even rehearse the replies to questions the employer might ask.

Design a portfolio. One of the most effective ways to impress an interviewer is to assemble all the facts about yourself and your career in a portfolio or scrapbook. Buy or make an oversize (22″ × 11″) album designed to conveniently display letter size and smaller documents, photos, clippings, and samples of your work. Subdivide the portfolio into personal, educational, work-related, and miscellaneous headings.

Let your imagination run free in designing the portfolio, especially if you're targeting an art-related career. To give you an idea of the kinds of material to include, here is a partial list of typical items:

- One good photo of yourself
- Diplomas (use photocopies)
- Certificates of completion of training courses
- Personal and professional references
- A sample printed piece that you contributed to. Explain alongside just what part you played in its production: typesetting, design, stripping, press, folding, or whatever. The sample should be unattached, so the interviewer may remove it from the portfolio for a closer look and feel.
- Newspaper and magazine clippings. These should be about work or nonwork-related areas, especially those that demonstrate achievement: winner of spelling bee, appointment to ROTC, Junior Achievement award, and other items of interest.

THE INTERVIEW

The interview is the last step of the job search. Depending on how well or badly you did in the course of the interview, you will be hired or you will hear, in effect, "Don't call us, we'll call you." It doesn't matter how slick your resume is, how experienced or competent you may be, or how well you know the vice-president, if you fail the interview, you fail to land the job.

Recognizing this, you should make every effort to project an image of the kind of person the interviewer is looking for to fill the position. Knowing what that image is will get you halfway through the door.

The following discussion is distilled from the author's many years of experience sitting on the other side of the desk from hundreds, if not thousands, of job applicants.

What to Do Before the Interview

You've been called for an interview scheduled for tomorrow. What can you do to prepare for it? You should have been doing most of your preparation some time ago, when you first began your job search, namely: assessed your skills, strengths and weaknesses, and memorized a few descriptive sentences about each. You already know the field you wish to work in, the intermediate job, and the ultimate goal. The resume and cover letter have already gone out, and your references and testimonials are neatly tucked into your job portfolio. Days ago, you filled out and mailed the application form.

But there's one thing you can't do until you know the identity of the firm: you should investigate, discreetly of course, the person who will be conducting the interview. Normally, a couple of phone calls will accomplish this for you. Try to unearth as much information about him or her that you might bring up in conversation. You flatter the interviewer by mentioning any relevant fact: an article he or she may have written, a recent promotion, election to office in a professional association. Not only do you flatter the interviewer, but you also prove to him or her that you have done your homework, establishing yourself as a resourceful person.

Dress the Part

How much weight does an interviewer give to appearance? It's hard to say, but of this you may be sure: Your appearance makes as much of an impression on the interviewer as your credentials. Long after you have left the office, your appearance will be remembered, your words forgotten.

No matter what position you may be applying for, you should dress as though you are applying for a front office job. If you're looking for a job as a press operator, don't come to the interview in work clothes. And don't overdress, either! If you dress so fancily that it makes *you* uncomfortable, it will do the same for the interviewer.

Keep this in mind when choosing your wardrobe—*avoid extremes.*

Be on Time

Not only does tardiness annoy the interviewer, who may be a very busy person, but it also forces you to apologize almost with your first breath. Apologizing puts you in a subservient position immediately, and the rest of the interview will suffer.

Plan to arrive at least half an hour before the scheduled interview. If all goes well and you haven't been held up by traffic, turn in at a coffee shop and relax for the next twenty minutes. If you have not eaten, have something light so you won't be distracted by hunger pangs. While you're relaxing, review the assets you have previously memorized.

At five minutes before the time, present yourself to the receptionist. Arriving too early puts pressure on the interviewer, which will be resented. As in all things, timing is of the essence.

What to Say and Do in the First Minute

Now comes the moment when, in all likelihood, a decision will be made whether you are a viable candidate for the job—the moment when you are face-to-face with the interviewer. There are two things you do—you stick out your hand, and you say something.

Whether you are a man or a woman, a handshake tells a great deal about you. Most probably, the interviewer has stood up behind the desk as you approach. Walk right up and take the offered hand, looking the person straight in the eye and smiling.

Avoid either a bone-crushing grip or a limp handshake. A firm handshake is best.

The interviewer already knows your name, but it doesn't hurt to repeat it. Say, "Hello, I'm Jay Stillwell (first and last name). It's a pleasure to meet you." Present yourself straightforwardly and with dignity. Show your respect for yourself, the interviewer, and the job being discussed.

Get Inside the Interviewer's Head

Once the introductions are over, you must strive to stay on the same level as the interviewer, technically and intellectually. Here are some tips that may help:

TRY TO LIKE THE INTERVIEWER

Everybody has good points that we can like. As you look over the interviewer, think to yourself, "There's a really kind person under that gruff exterior." Or, "This is someone who really knows the job." If you genuinely like someone, you will exert an influence, and before you know it, you have established a mutual respect for each other. From the interviewer's point of view, it's difficult to hire someone you dislike, regardless of qualifications.

DEVELOP ENTHUSIASM

You can show your enthusiasm by expressing an interest in the company, the job, and the latest developments in printing. If you have done your homework, you can bring up some facts you have learned about the company at this time. Don't overdo it, though; and don't appear falsely eager. State what genuinely interests you. The interviewer knows that enthusiasm for the job, the company, and the people we work with is a valuable, and scarce, quality in employees.

BE FAMILIAR WITH THE JARGON OF PRINTING

One indicator of how advanced you are in your field, regardless of the technology, is your familiarity with the words and phrases in common use. Jargon is useful in all fields—it would take a lot of words to describe baseball's double play, for example. Study the glossary, Appendix E, if you are not already familiar with the words.

ADMIRE SOMETHING ABOUT THE INTERVIEWER... WITH CAUTION

Without giving the impression of currying favor, an expression of admiration is appropriate if it is sincerely felt and well deserved. *Don't admire* the person's taste in clothes—that's too personal. Admire instead the interviewer's professional accomplishments, if you know them beforehand, such as a well-written article or the quality of a printed sample on the wall.

DON'T LIE

Lying will get you nowhere, because lies about previous experience or education are easily checked for accuracy—and they will be checked. If you don't know something, offer an honest admission and clearly state your willingness or aptitude to learn.

Questions You Will Be Asked

It's impossible to predict exactly what questions you will be asked during an interview, but here are a number of questions (and possible answers) that are popular with interviewers.

WHY DO YOU WANT TO WORK FOR US?

Your answer: "Because I have done some research on your company, and I believe you offer me the kind of opportunity I want to advance myself technically. I like your pre-press department and the state-of-the-art equipment you use. And I especially want the challenge of four-color work, which you do a lot of."

IF WE HIRED YOU, WHERE WOULD YOU WANT TO BE TEN YEARS DOWN THE ROAD?

Your answer: "Vice president in charge of production." (Aim high—you won't hit anybody.) If the interviewer *is* the vice president in charge of production, so much the better. However, don't cite a job that would be on a higher level than the interviewer's. And don't say flat-out, "Your job," because that is threatening.

APART FROM MONEY, WHAT WILL YOU EXPECT TO GET OUT OF THIS JOB?

Your answer: "The satisfaction of doing a job well and gaining some recognition. I believe that I can bring to any printing job my ability to do things right. I am a stickler for exactness, and the type of work you do requires my kind of accuracy."

WHY SHOULD I RECOMMEND YOU FOR THE JOB?

Your answer: "I know you're looking for long-term relationships with your employees, so I'm the person you would want. I'm a steady, dependable worker and I won't be job hopping."

DESCRIBE THREE ACHIEVEMENTS IN YOUR SCHOOL OR WORK CAREER

Careful! Your answer should have been prepared in advance for this one, a favorite of employment professionals. The achievements you think most noteworthy could tell a lot about you. Some safe achievements: election to some office in a student or professional association; straight A's; completion of a four-year course in three; perfect attendance; first-place award in speed typing, design competition, debating, 4H, or similar contests; special accomplishments on the job that increased your company's production.

**OUR COMPANY INSISTS ON PUNCTUALITY.
HOW DO YOU FEEL ABOUT THAT?**

Your answer: "I developed the habit in school to get to my class at least 10 minutes before the bell rang. It gave me a chance to organize my thinking. That would not be a problem with me." If punctuality has not been your strong suit in the past, don't say so directly. Instead, just respond, "Being at work on time is simply part of the job, and I would want to arrive and settle in before the workday begins."

**HOW DO I KNOW YOU'RE THE KIND
OF PERSON YOU SAY YOU ARE?**

Your answer: "Here are my references. I think you can believe what they say if you would take the trouble to call them."

**TELL ME ABOUT YOUR
STRENGTHS AND WEAKNESSES**

Your answer: "My strengths lie in the areas of _____ and _____. I did well in both in technical school. However, I didn't do so well in _____ and _____. (I can't draw a straight line; I'm not good at foreign languages.)" Be honest about your weaknesses, but don't leave the interviewer with the notion that you're hopeless. Follow up with, "But I'm working on it." Sometimes you can even cite as a weakness a quality an employer might view as an asset: "I'm a real perfectionist."

ARE THERE KINDS OF PEOPLE YOU LIKE OR DISLIKE?

The interviewer will pay careful attention to your answer, because it has many implications. You be just as careful with your answer. "Basically, I like everybody, unless a person proves to be untrustworthy." Your likes and dislikes reflect your own worthiness.

HOW DO YOU FEEL ABOUT
WORKING AGAINST A DEADLINE?

Your answer: "I'm used to deadlines. In my previous job, I never missed a deadline in four years." Be truthful, and state your case simply and directly to get the point across that you are dependable. If you have blown deadlines in the past, don't volunteer this information (but don't deny it if you're directly asked). You could honestly say, "I know that deadlines are important, and I understand that I would be expected to meet them."

TELL ME ABOUT THE BOOKS YOU HAVE READ RECENTLY,
ANY MOVIE YOU HAVE SEEN, AND
THE KIND OF MUSIC YOU LIKE

This question is designed to look at your personality, tastes, or intellect. If you haven't read any books lately, be truthful. If you say you have read some, the interviewer might ask you to name them. Just put your best foot forward. If you regularly read nonfiction, see only the best movies, and have an interest in music, any music, be sure to say so. If you subscribe to professional or trade magazines, or read other material that relates directly to your work, mention it. If these sorts of cultural activities don't appeal to you, try to mention what does: "I don't see a lot of films because I like to spend my spare time working on my car (or tending my garden, or sewing, or doing volunteer work in the community)."

Questions That You Should Ask...and Not Ask

After you and the interviewer have chatted for a while and the interview is almost at an end, the interviewer often will ask, "Do you have any questions?" Assuming that you already have been given the details of salary, bonus, hours, vacation, and similar items, this is an opportunity for you to evaluate whether the job is really what you are looking for. To find out, ask some searching questions.

WOULD YOU MIND TELLING ME ABOUT
THE PERSON I WOULD REPORT TO?

You'll want to know the person's name, title, and how many people report to the same person. You also would hope to find out what kind of person the supervisor is, prior to a face-to-face meeting. There's nothing like advance planning.

WHAT KIND OF RELATIONSHIP DOES
THE COMPANY HAVE WITH ITS EMPLOYEES?

If the relationships are good and mutually respectful, the answers will be straightforward. If the answers appear contradictory or vague, chances are that relationships are strained. There must be a reason.

DO I RECEIVE ANY EXTRA COMPENSATION
FOR SUPERIOR JOB PERFORMANCE?

This tells the interviewer that you are setting your sights above and beyond the ordinary performance of duty.

HOW HAS THE COMPANY PROGRESSED
IN THE PAST YEAR?

Good question, because it reflects your interest in the company's welfare, instead of just your own. Also, if the company is on the ropes, you may have to be looking elsewhere for a job.

QUESTIONS YOU SHOULD NOT ASK

Try to avoid "why" questions—they can be very hard to answer and the interviewer may resent them.

The strategy of your questioning mainly is to advance your image in the eyes of the interviewer. Asking astute, intelligent questions will help to impress the interviewer that you are a serious contender for the job.

Using a Portfolio

If you have a portfolio of samples of your work, this is your show-and-tell act, following your conversation with the interviewer. Keep the portfolio out of the way during the interview. At the appropriate moment, you can say something like, "May I show you some samples I have assembled here?"

You should try to stand alongside of the interviewer while *you* turn the pages, and comment on the samples. You should have rehearsed relevant and useful items to point out as you *slowly* turn the pages. If the interviewer has a comment, pause in turning the pages while you respond.

When the interview is ended, offer to leave the portfolio behind, but make a definite appointment for retrieving it. This gives you a chance at a second interview—a sure sign that things are going your way.

Send a Follow-Up Letter

Always send a thank-you letter. Mail it the same day as the interview if possible:

Dear Mr. [or Ms.] Johnson:

Thank you again for the opportunity to present my credentials today. I enjoyed meeting you and your colleagues.

Our discussion confirmed my belief that I would make a valuable addition to your staff of workers. I was especially impressed with the efficiency with which your groups handles the publication of so many periodicals. I would be proud to be a part of your team.

I was not aware that you have a close relationship with the Hickory Tech College; please feel free to contact Dr. Pat Lowery of the Graphic Arts Department for any further information you may want about my abilities.

Thank you again, and I look forward to a future meeting with you in the very near future.

Sincerely,

Lee Wharton

SAMPLE RESUMES AND COVER LETTER

Sample Resume of a Recent Vocational School Graduate

Charles N. Harrison
304 West Church Road
Arlington, VA 20405

Telephone (302) 555-8998

Objective: To secure a position as a press operator with an established firm with opportunities for professional growth.

EXPERIENCE

1995–97 Enrolled in on-the-job work/school program at Metro Vocational, affiliated with Acme Printing Company, Washington, D.C.

Assisted in operation of 14 x 20 and 22 x 29 presses. Also worked in platemaking department three months.

1991–95 Summer job with Arlington School Board and part time during winter months. Assisted vocational guidance counselor. Operated duplicator press, small Baumfolder.

EDUCATION

1995–97 Metro Vocational-Technical School, Reston, VA
Certificate of Completion

1991–95 Arlington High School, Arlington, VA
Vocational Courses, Diploma

REFERENCES

Available upon request.

Sample Resume of an Experienced Printing Sales Person

MARIAN HUTCHINS
140 Franklin Drive
Northwood, NJ 08105
Home: (609) 555-7737
Work: (609) 555-3373
E-mail: HutchinsM@mymail.com

WORK EXPERIENCE

1990–present **Jonesboro Printing Corporation, Brooklyn, NY**
Senior Cost Estimator
Directed cost estimating group for a $10 million printing corporation. Set new protocols and criteria for determining costs. Developed templates in MS Excel spreadsheets for corporate use, resulting in 93 percent accuracy, a 230 percent increase in accuracy and cost controls. Interfaced with senior management, print sales team, and vendors. Monitored costs, and maintained overhead and profit ratios.

Joined Jonesboro in 1990 as a cost estimator trainee. Promoted to cost estimator in 1992; became department head in November 1993.

1988–90 **Seaside Offset Press, Cape May, NJ**
Customer Service Representative
Prepared rough and comprehensive layouts for printing customers, assisted in the stripping department, operated the Autologic APS Micro-composer.

1981–88	**Bold, Bursten & Gramercy, Ocean City, N.J. advertising agency**
	Pasteup artist

SPECIAL SKILLS

Computer: Word Processing, Spreadsheets (Excel and Lotus), Internet research, ccMail. Estimating: Strong knowledge of industry benchmarks, terminology, and vendor lists Strong Interpersonal skills

EDUCATION

| 1979 | BA, Art, Philadelphia College. Minor in Lettering |
| 1991 | Course in bookkeeping and marketing, Brooklyn College |

REFERENCES

Available upon request.

Sample Cover Letter

[Return address—name optional]
[Date]

Ms. Joan Havershire
City Service Press, Inc.
53 Venture Highway
Philadelphia, PA 19108

Dear Ms. Havershire:

I am writing in response to your advertisement for a customer service supervisor in this morning's *Patriot.* Enclosed is my resume.

The position advertised is of special interest to me because of my experience, which is similar to the duties outlined in the ad.

I believe I am especially qualified because of my work with customers in my previous employment at Cape May Offset Press.

In my capacity as customer service representative, I was responsible for planning, designing, and producing a wide variety of printing jobs, including four-color work. I am familiar with all stages of pre-press work.

I would be happy to meet with you at your convenience.

May I call you early next week?

Sincerely,

Marian Hutchins

CHAPTER 7

A FINAL WORD

From the time of the European monks of the Middle Ages and their exquisite hand-lettering, to the Gutenberg invention of the fifteenth century, to today's state-of-the-art, computer-operated wonder presses, the world of the printer has occupied a special place in the imaginations of people worldwide. Its aura comes from the art of communication, from an outreach that has grown in influence and vitality with each new decade.

Today, the world of print communication knows no boundaries. The sophisticated technologies of the medium are like a train at the station, waiting for a new generation of communicators to set the pace, move minds, and shape the future. I heartily recommend that you get the education and experiences you need to get on board…and while we can't "hold the presses" for you, there's a wonderful track for you to travel up ahead. Reach for it. You'll have a trip.

COLLEGE AND UNIVERSITY PROGRAMS

This compilation draws together a number of sources, including college directories, university publications, and Internet directory searches. Not included are college programs that deal exclusively with graphic design. The focus here is the technical and business components of the printing industries, including pre-press, bindery, and electronic reprographic specialties. Undoubtedly, a handful of reputable programs will have been omitted accidentally, so the reader is advised to consult with current college directories, which are published annually.

As with all compilations such as this, it is best to identify a short-list of possibilities and write directly to the institution in question for additional information.

Alabama

Alabama Agricultural and Mechanical University
Bessemer State Technical College
Bishop State Community College, Mobile
Chattahoochee Valley Community College
Community College of the Air Force
J. F. Drake State Technical College
John M. Patterson State Technical College

Southwest State Technical College, Mobile
University of Alabama

Arizona

Al Collins Graphic Design School
Maricopa Skill Center, Gateway Community College
Pima Community College

Arkansas

Arkansas State University, Jonesboro
Petit Jean Technical College
Phillips County Community College
Southern Arkansas University

California

Advertising Arts College
Allan Hancock College
American River College
Antelope Vale College
Bakersfield College
Butte College
California Polytechnic State University
Chaffey Community College
City College of San Francisco
Compton College
Courtesy Printing/School of Printing
El Camino College
Evergreen Valley College
Fashion Institute of Design and Merchandising
Fresno City College
Fullerton College
Golden West College
Laney College, Oakland

Long Beach City College
Los Angeles Trade and Technical College
Mission College
Modesto Junior College
Moopark College
MTI–Western Business College
Palomar College
Rio Hondo College
Riverside Community College
Sacramento City College
San Joaquin Delta College
Santa Barbara City College
Santa Monica College
Silicon Valley College
Ventura College

Colorado

Aims Community College
Boulder Tech Educational Center
Community College of Aurora
Denver Institute of Technology
Front Range Community College
Mesa College Area Vocational School
Mesa State College
Pikes Peak Community College
Platt College

Connecticut

Gateway Community–Technical College

District of Columbia

Howard University
University of the District of Columbia

Florida

Brevard Community College
D. G. Erwin Technical Center
Daytona Beach Community College
Florida Community College at Jacksonville
Fred K. Marchman Vocational–Technical Center
Lewis M. Lively Area Vocational–Technical Center
Miami–Dade Community College
Miami Lakes Technical Education Center
North Technical Educational Center
Okaloosa–Walton Community College
Palm Beach Community College
Pensacola Junior College
Polk Community College
Radford M. Locklin Vocational–Technical Center
Santa Fe Community College
Schwettman Adult Education Center
St. Augustine Technical Center
St. Petersburg Junior College, Clearwater
Valencia Community College

Georgia

Albany Tech Institute
Atlanta Area Technical Institute
Atlanta Metropolitan College
Augusta Technical Institute
Chattahoochee Technical Institute
Columbus Technical Institute
DeKalb Technical Institute
Macon Technical Institute

Idaho

Idaho State University
Lewis & Clark State College

Illinois

Belleville Area College
City College of Chicago
College of DuPage
Elgin Community College
Kennedy–King College
Lewis & Clark Community College
Moraine Valley Community College
South Suburban College
Triton College

Indiana

Ball State University
Indiana State University, Terre Haute
Indiana Vocational College, Ivy Tech Wabash Valley
Vincennes University

Iowa

Colby Community College
Des Moines Area Community College
Eastern Iowa Community College, Davenport
Iowa Lakes Community College
Iowa Western Community College
Kirkwood Community College
Northeast Kansas Area Vocational/Technical School
University of Northern Iowa

Kansas

Flint Hills Technical School
Fort Scott Community College
Haskell Indian Junior College

Hutchinson Community College
Kansas City Area Vocational–Technical School
Manhattan Area Technical Center

Kentucky

Bowling Green State Vocational–Technical School
Jefferson Community College
Kentucky Tech, Jefferson Campus
Kentucky Tech, Mayo Campus
Kentucky Tech, Somerset Campus
Mayo State Vocational–Technical School
Morehead State University
Murray State University

Maine

Central Maine Technical College

Maryland

Catonsville Community College
Columbia Union College
Montgomery College, Rockville Campus

Massachusetts

Assabet Valley Regional Vocational–Technical School
Bunker Hill Community College
Middlesex Community College, Bedford
North Bennet Street School
Northern Essex Community College
Springfield Technical Community College

Michigan

Alpena Community College
Andrews University

Ferris State University
Gogebic Community College, Ironwood
Grand Rapids Community College
Henry Ford Community College
Lansing Community College
Macomb Community College, Warren
Madonna University
Muskegon Community College
Northern Michigan University
Northwestern Michigan College
Oakland Community College
Washtenaw Community College
Western Michigan University

Minnesota

Dunwoody Industrial Institute
Hennepin Technical College

Mississippi

Central Missouri State University
College of the Ozarks
East Mississippi Community College
Hinds Community College
Joe Herndon Area Vocational–Technical School
Mississippi Delta Community College
Mississippi Valley State College
Northwest Mississippi Community College
NS Hillyard Area Vocational–Technical School
St. Louis Community College–Florissant Valley
St. Louis Community College–Forest Park

Missouri

Cape Girardeau Area Vocational–Technical School

Montana

Miles Community College

Nebraska

Central Community College
Central Community College–Hastings Campus
Lincoln School of Commerce
Metropolitan Community College, Ft. Omaha
Southeast Community College–Lincoln Campus

Nevada

Community College of Southern Nevada
Truckee Meadows Community College

New Hampshire

New Hampshire Technical College: Laconia

New Jersey

Bergen Community College
Burlington County College
Cumberland County Area Vocational Tech
Cumberland Tech Educational Center
Ocean County Area Vocational–Technical Schools
Salem County Vocational–Technical Career Center

New Mexico

Southwestern Indian Polytechnic Institute

New York

Corning Community College
Erie Community College, North
Mohawk Valley Community College
New York Technical College
Rochester Institute of Technology
SUNY College of Technology, Farmingdale

North Carolina

Alamance Community College
Appalachian State University
Central Piedmont Community College
Chowan College
Forsyth Technical Community College
Lenoir Community College
McDowell Technical Community College

North Dakota

North Dakota State College of Science

Ohio

Auburn Career Center
Columbus State Community College
Lourdes College
Owens Community College
Sinclair Community College

Oklahoma

Central Oklahoma Vocational–Technical College
Northeastern Oklahoma
Northeastern State University
Oklahoma City Community College
Oklahoma State University, Okmulgee

Oregon

Linn–Benton Community College
Mount Hood Community College
Portland Community College

Pennsylvania

Altoona Area Vocational–Technical School
Art Institute of Pittsburgh
Bucks County Community College
California University of Pennsylvania
Community College of Allegheny County
Graphic Arts Education Center
Hiram G. Andrews Center
Hussian School of Art
La Roche College
Luzerne County Community College
Mercer County Area Vocational–Technical School
Pennsylvania College of Technology
Thaddeus Stevens State School of Technology
University of the Arts
West Chester University of Pennsylvania
Westmoreland County Community College

South Carolina

Midlands Technical College, Columbia
Midlands Technical College
Trident Technical College

South Dakota

Southeast Technical Institute

Tennessee

Memphis College of Art
Morristown State Area Vocational–Technical School
Nashville State Technical Institute
State Technical Institute, Memphis
Tennessee Technology Center at Memphis

Texas

American Trade Institute
College of the Mainland
Collin County Community College District
East Texas State University
Eastfield College
Houston Community College
Kilgore College
Kingwood College
Lee College
Midland College
Montgomery Community College District
Navarro College
North Harris College
Printing Industries of the Gulf Coast–Technical Training Center
Tarrant County Junior College
Texas Southern University
Texas State Technical College at Waco
Tyler Junior College

Utah

Dixie College
Salt Lake City Community College

Virginia

Danville Community College

John Tyler Community College
Patrick Henry Community College
Virginia Intermont College

Washington

Art Institute of Seattle
Highline Community College
Seattle Central Community College
Seattle Central Community College
Shoreline Community College
Spokane Community College
Walla Walla College

West Virginia

West Virginia Institute of Technology

Wisconsin

Clover Park Vocational Technical Institute
Fox Valley Technical College
Lakeshore Technical College
Madison Area Technical College
Mid–State Technical College
Milwaukee Area Technical College
Moraine Park Technical College
North Central Technical College
Tidewater Community College
Western Wisconsin Technical College, La Crosse

Wyoming

Northwest College

NATIONAL PRINTING AND ALLIED INDUSTRIES ASSOCIATIONS (UNITED STATES AND CANADA)

The following associations will supply you with employment and other essential information in their respective fields. Many of them also offer scholarship information. For a complete list of printing scholarships, write to the Education Council of the Graphic Arts Industry listed below. Websites are given for associations, wherever possible.

American Business Press
  675 Third Avenue
  New York, NY 10017-5704
  http://www.abp2.com/

American Institute of Graphic Arts
  164 Fifth Avenue
  New York, NY 10010
  http://www.aiga.org/

American Newspaper Publishers Association
  The Newspaper Center
  11600 Sunrise Valley Drive
  Reston, VA 22091
  http://www.ipac.net/ir/adassoc12.html

American Paper Institute
  260 Madison Avenue
  New York, NY 10016

American Printing History Association
  P. O. Box 4922
  Grand Central Station, NY 10163-4922
  http://wally.rit.edu/cary/apha.html

American Quick Printing Association
  1324 W. Clay
  Houston, TX 77019

Association of College and University Printers (ACUP)
  Lehigh University
  Mountaintop Campus
  118 Atlas Drive
  Building J
  Bethlehem, PA 18015

Binding and Finishers Association
  408 Eighth Avenue
  Suite 10A
  New York, NY 10001-1816
  http://www.bindernet.com/bfa.htm

Binding Industries of America
  70 E. Lake Street
  Chicago, IL 60601-5907
  http://www.bindernet.com/hpbia.htm

Business Forms Management Association (BFMA)
  319 S.W. Washington Street
  Suite 710
  Portland, OR 97204
  http://www.bfma.org/~bfma/

Canadian Printing Industries Association
  75 Albert Street
  Suite 906
  Ottawa, Ontario
  Canada
  K1P 5E7
  http://www.capitalnet.com/~printing

Digital Printing and Imaging Association
  10015 Main Street
  Fairfax, VA 22031-3489
  http://www.dpia.org/

Direct Marketing Association
  1120 Avenue of the Americas
  New York, NY 10036-6700
  http://www.the-dma.org/

Document Management Industries Association
  (formerly National Business Forms Association)
  433 E. Monroe Avenue
  Alexandria, VA 22301
  http://www.dmia.com/

Education Council of the Graphic Arts Industry
  NPES—The Association for Suppliers of Printing and Publishing
    Technologies
  Attn: Ms. JoAnne Laffey, Administrator
  Reston, VA 20191-4367
  http://www.npes.org/industry.html#education

Engineering Reprographic Society
  P.O. Box 202121
  Bloomington, MN 55420

Engraved Stationery Manufacturers Association, Inc.
  305 Plus Park Boulevard
  Nashville, TN 37217-1005

Fibre Box Assocation
2850 Golf Road
Rolling Meadows, IL 60008-4050

Flexographic Technical Association
900 Marconi Avenue
Ronkonkoma, NY 11779
http://www.fta-ffta.org/

Graphic Arts Association
1900 Cherry Street
Philadelphia, PA 19103
http://www.gaa1900.com/index.html

Graphic Arts Education and Research Foundation
NPES—The Association for Suppliers of Printing and Publishing
Technologies
Attn: Ms. JoAnne Laffey, Administrator
Reston, VA 20191-4367
http://www.npes.org/industry.html#research

Graphic Arts Employers of America
c/o Printing Industries of America, Inc.
100 Daingerfield Road
Alexandria, VA 22314-2888
http://www.printing.org/

Graphic Arts Marketing Information Service
100 Daingerfield Road
Alexandria, VA 22314-2888
http://www.printing.org/gamabout.htm

Graphic Arts Technical Foundation
200 Deer Run Road
Sewickley, PA 15143-2600
http://www.gatf.lm.com/

Graphic Communications Association
  100 Daingerfield Road
  Alexandria, VA 22314-2888
  http://www.gca.org/

Gravure Association of America
  1200A Scottsville Road
  Rochester, NY 14624
  http://www.gaa.org/

Institute of Paper Science and Technology
  500 10th Street, N.W.
  Atlanta, GA 30318
  http://www.ipst.edu/

International Association for Document & Information Management
      Solutions
  2111 Wilson Boulevard
  Suite 350
  Arlington, VA 22201
  http://www.ibfi.org/

International Association of Printing House Craftsmen
  7042 Brooklyn Boulevard
  Minneapolis, MN 55429
  http://www.iaphc.org

International Microelectronics and Packaging Society
  1850 Centennial Park Drive
  Suite 105
  Reston, VA 20191
  http://www.ishm.ee.vt.edu/

International Prepress Association
  7200 France Avenue S.
  Suite 327
  Edina, MN 55435
  http://www.ipa.org

International Thermographers Association
  100 Daingerfield Road
  Alexandria, VA 22314-2888
  http://www.printing.org/ita.htm

Label Printing Industries of America
  100 Daingerfield Road
  Alexandria, VA 22314-2888
  http://www.printing.org/label.htm

National Association of Litho Clubs
  6550 Don Joy Drive
  Cincinnati, OH 45242

National Association of Printers and Lithographers
  780 Palisade Avenue
  Teaneck, NJ 07666
  http://www.napl.org/

National Association of Printing Ink Manufacturers
  Heights Plaza
  777 Terrace Avenue
  Hasbrouck Heights, NJ 07604
  http://www.napim.org/

National Association of Quick Printers
  401 N. Michigan Avenue
  Chicago, IL 60611
  http://www.naqp.org/

National Paper Trade Association
  111 Great Neck Road
  Great Neck, NY 11021

North American Graphic Arts Suppliers Association
  1720 Florida Avenue N.W.
  Washington, DC, 20009-2660

NPES—The Association For Suppliers of Printing & Publishing
  Technologies
  1899 Preston White Drive
  Reston, VA 20191-4367
  http://www.npes.org/

Paper Industry Management Association
  1699 Wall Street
  Suite 212
  Mt Prospect, IL 60056-5782
  http://PIMA-online.org/

The Printer's Form
  P.O. Box 5491
  Anderson, South Carolina 29623-5491
  http://www.vais.com/forum/

Printing Industries of America, Inc.
  100 Daingerfield Road
  Alexandria, VA 22314-2888
  http://www.printing.org

Screen Printing Technical Foundation
  10015 Main Street
  Fairfax, VA 22031-3403
  http://www.sgia.org/sptfover.html

Screenprinting and Graphic Imaging Association
  10015 Main Street
  Fairfax, VA 22031-3489
  http://www.sgia.org/

The Silk & Rayon Printers & Dyers Association of America
  1301 Charles Street
  Point Pleasant, NJ 08742
  http://www.srpda.org/

Society for Imaging Science and Technology
    7003 Kilworth Lane
    Springfield, VA 22151
    http://www.imaging.org/

Tag and Label Manufacturer's Institute
    1330 W. 49th Street
    Davenport, IA 52806-3666

Technical Association of the Pulp and Paper Industry
    Technology Park/Atlanta
    P.O. Box 105113
    Atlanta, GA 30348-5113
    http://www.tappi.org/

Typographers International Association
    2262 Hall Place, N.W.
    Washington, DC 20007

U.S. Screen Printing Institute
    605 S. Rockford Drive
    Tempe, AZ 85281-3016
    http://www.usscreen.com/

Waterless Printing Association
    P.O. Box 59800
    Chicago, IL 60645
    http://www.waterless.org/

LOCAL ORGANIZATIONS AND REGIONAL AFFILIATES OF PRINTING INDUSTRIES OF AMERICA

Many regional printing associations offer free employment services. They will inform their member firms about your availability for employment. Many of the regional associations are affiliates of the Printing Industries of America, Inc., while others are independent organizations dedicated to serving business in their areas. This compilation is merely a sampling of regional organizations, as a number of fine organizations were not included owing to their service to small communities or regions.

California

Printing Industries Association, Inc. of Southern California
    1434 W. 12th Street
    Los Angeles, CA 90015
    (213) 747-5521
    http://www.piasc.org/

Printing Industries Association of San Diego
    3914 Murphy Canyon Road
    Suite A–107
    San Diego, CA 92123
    (619) 571-6555
    http://www.dwmi.com/creative/pia/cr_pia1.html

Printing Industries of Northern California
  665 Third Street
  Suite 500
  San Francisco, CA 94107-1990
  http://www.pinc.org/

Printing & Imaging Association Mountain States
  5031 S. Ulster Street #350
  Denver, Colorado 80237
  http://www.sni.net/piams/

Connecticut

Printing Industry Association of Connecticut & Western
      Massachusetts
  One Regency Drive
  P.O. Box 30
  Bloomfield, CT 06002

The Printing Industry of Connecticut, Inc.
  P.O. Box 144
  Milford, CT 06460

Florida

Printing Industries of Florida
  2233 Lee Road
  Suite 217
  Executive Square
  Winter Park, FL 32789
  http://www.pwr.com/printpaf/

Georgia

Printing Association of Georgia
  5020 Highlands Parkway
  Smyrna, GA 30082
  http://www.piag.org/

Illinois

Printing Industry of Illinois/Indiana Association
  70 E. Lake Street
  Chicago, IL 60601

Iowa

Printing Industry of the Midlands, Inc.
  4430 114th Street
  Urbandale, IA 50322

Kansas

Printing Industries Association of the Heartland
  250 Richards Road
  Suite 267
  Kansas City, MO 64116

Maryland

Printing Industries of Maryland
  2045 York Road
  Timonium, MD 21093
  http://www.printmd.com/

Massachusetts

Printing Industries of New England
10 Tech Circle
Natick, MA 01760
http://www.pine.org/

Michigan

Printing Industries of Michigan
23815 Northwestern Highway
Suite 2700
Southfield, MI 48075-7713

Minnesota

Printing Industry of Minnesota, Inc.
2829 University Avenue, S.E.
Suite 750
Minneapolis, MN 55414-3222

Missouri

Printing Industries of St. Louis
The Joseph White Building
1790 S. Brentwood Boulevard
St. Louis, MO 63144

Printing Industries Association of Kansas City
250 N.W. Richards Road
Kansas City, MO 64116-4275

New York

Association of the Graphic Communications
330 Seventh Avenue
9th Floor
New York, NY 10001-5010

Printing Industries Association of New York State, Inc.
   636 N. French Road
   Suite 1
   Amherst, NY 14228

North Carolina

The Printing Industry of the Carolinas, Inc.
   3601 Rose Lake Drive
   Charlotte, NC 28217-2813
   http://www.picanet.org/

Ohio

Printing Industries Association of Northern Ohio, Inc.
   30400 Detroit Road
   Suite 206
   Cleveland, OH 44145

Printing Industries Association of Southern Ohio
   1371 Glendale-Milford Road
   Cincinnati, OH 45215

Printing Industry of Central Ohio
   88 Dorchester Square
   P.O. Box 819
   Westerville, OH 43086-0819

Oklahoma

Graphic Communications Industries Association of Oklahoma, Inc.
   P.O. Box 691407
   Tulsa, OK 74169

Oregon

Pacific Printing and Imaging Association
5319 S.W. Westgate Drive
Suite 117
Portland, OR 97221-2488
(See also under Washington)
http://www.ppi-assoc.org/

Tennessee

The Printing Industry Association of the South, Inc.
P.O. Box 290249
Nashville, TN 37229

Texas

Printing Industries Association of Texas
910 W. Mockingbird Lane
Suite 200
Dallas, TX 75247-5174
http://www.azone.net/pia-texas/

Printing Industries of the Gulf Coast, Inc.
1324 W. Clay Street
Houston, TX 77019

Utah

Printing Industries of Utah
445 E. Second, S.
Suite 16
Salt Lake City, UT 84111

Virginia

Printing Industries of Virginia, Inc.
  1108 E. Main Street
  Suite 300
  Richmond, VA 23219

Washington

Pacific Printing and Imaging Association
  180 Nickerson
  Suite 102
  Seattle, WA 98109-1631
  (See also under Oregon)
  http://www.ppi-assoc.org/

Wisconsin

Printing Industries of Wisconsin
  P.O. Box 126
  Elm Grove, WI 53122

Canada

Association Des Arts Graphiques Du Québec
  65, rue de Castelnau ouest
  Bureau 101
  Montréal, Québec
  Canada
  H2R 2W3

The British Columbia Printing Industries Association (BCPIA)
    409 Granville Street
    Suite 523
    Vancouver, B.C.
    Canada
    V6C 1T2

The Nova Scotia Printing Industries Association
    P.O. Box 82
    Enfield, Nova Scotia
    Canada
    B2T 1C6

The Ontario Printing and Imaging Association
    6420 Kestrel Road
    Mississauga, Ontario
    Canada
    L5T 1Z7
    http://www.opia.com

The Printing and Graphics Industries Association of Alberta (PGIA)
    P.O. Box 21006
    Dominion Postal Outlet
    Calgary, Alberta
    Canada
    T2P 4H5

The Saskatchewan Graphic Arts Industries Association (SGAIA)
    P.O. Box 7152
    Saskatoon, Saskatchewan
    Canada
    S7K 4J1d

TRADE PUBLICATIONS

AIGA Graphics Design USA
    1695 Oak Street
    Lakewood, NJ 09701

AIGA Journal of Graphic Design
    American Institute of Graphic Arts
    164 Fifth Avenue
    New York, NY 10010–5900

APHA Letter
    American Printing History Association
    Box 4922
    Grand Central Station
    New York, NY 10163

ATF Newsletter
    American Typecasting Fellowship
    Box 263
    Terra Alta, WV 26764

American Ink Maker
    29 N. Wacker Drive
    Chicago, IL 60606

American Printer
  c/o Intertec Publishing Corporation
  9800 Metcalf Avenue
  Overland Park, KS 66202

Canadian Printer
  777 Bay Street
  Toronto, Ontario
  Canada
  M5W 1A7

Flexo
  c/o Flexographic Technical Association
  900 Marconi Avenue
  Ronkonkoma, NY 11779

Form Magazine
  Document Management Industries Association
  433 E. Monroe Avenue
  Alexandria, VA 22301

Graphic Arts Monthly
  245 W. 17th Street
  New York, NY 10011

Graphic Arts Product News
  300 W. Adams Street
  Chicago, IL 60606

Electronic Publishing
  P. O. Box 1260
  Tulsa, OK 74101

High Volume Printing
  P.O. Box 7280
  Libertyville, IL 60048–7280

In-House Graphics
    United Communications Group
    11300 Rockville Pike
    Suite 1100
    Rockville, MD 20852–3030

In-Plant Printer
    P.O. Box 7280
    Libertyville, IL 60048–7280

In-Plant Reproductions
    P.O. Box 7280
    Libertyville, IL 60048–7280

Ink On Paper
    Graphic Arts Publishing Company
    3100 Bronson Hill Road
    Livonia, NY 14487–9716

Instant and Small Commercial Printer
    P.O. Box 7280
    Libertyville, IL 60048–7280

Modern Reprographics
    1017 Wenonah Avenue
    Oak Park, IL 60304–1812

New England Printer and Publisher
    12 Carleton Drive
    Box 810
    Newburyport, MA 01950

Paper, Film and Foil Converter
    29 N. Wacker Drive
    Chicago, IL 60606–3203

Paperboard Packaging
    131 W. 1st Street
    Duluth, MN 55802–2065

Prepress Bulletin
    552 W. 167th Street
    South Holland, IL 60473

Presspective
    737 Morray Street
    L.G.M. Graphics, Inc.
    Winnipeg, MB
    Canada
    R3J 9Z9

Print-Equip News
    E. N. Publishers
    215 Allen Avenue
    Box 5340
    Glendale, CA 91209–5540

Printing History
    American Printing History Association
    Box 4922
    Grand Central Station
    New York, NY 10163

Printing News
    249 W. 17th Street
    New York, NY 10011–5300

Printing Business Report
    National Association Printers & Lithographers
    780 Palisades Avenue
    Teaneck, NJ 07666

Printing Impressions
  North American Publishing Company
  401 N. Broad Street
  Philadelphia, PA 19108

Screen Printing
  407 Gilbert Avenue
  Cincinnati, OH 45202–2220

The Typographer
  2262 Hall Place, N.W.
  Washington, DC 20007–1865

Typographical Journal
  P.O. Box 2341
  Colorado Springs, CO 80901

GLOSSARY

The following words and terms are some of the more common ones used by printers. This is not a complete list. Some of the more technical terms have been omitted.

Accordion fold. Two or more parallel folds that alternate in direction like the pleats of an accordion.

Against the grain. In folding, a fold at a right angle to the direction of the paper grain.

Airbrush. A gun used by artists to spray color on a painting under the pressure of compressed air.

Antique finish. A paper term describing a rough, natural surface, as opposed to a glossy finish.

Apprentice. A person who is enrolled in a specified course of instruction leading to employment as a journeyman or woman under trade standards of practice. One who works under an agreement to serve an employer during a specified training period.

Art work. In printing, that part of the pre-press phase in which drawings, paintings, and photos are prepared for printing. The term also is used to describe the actual drawing, painting, or photo or the assembled flat.

Author's alterations. Changes in the original manuscript that occur after the type has been set. The term is used to distinguish them from changes necessitated by typographical errors. AA's are not usually considered the financial responsibility of the typesetter.

Backup. In presswork, printing on the second side of a sheet that is to be printed on both sides.

Backbone. The area of a book cover connecting the front and back covers. Also called a **Spine.**

Back lining. In book printing, a paper or fabric lining of the backbone, usually glued.

Basis weight. The weight in pounds of a ream (500 sheets) of paper cut to a specified size.

Bearer. In photoengraving, the metal left on a printing plate's borders to protect the printing surfaces during the process of molding. In composition, type-high slugs locked up inside a chase to protect the printing surface. In presswork, the surface-to-surface ends of cylinders that come into contact with each other.

Benday. A method of laying a screen on artwork or film to obtain various tones and shading.

Bimetallic plate. Lithographic plate made from two metals, the printing area being made from copper and the nonprinting area made from nickel, chromium, or stainless steel. The nonprinting areas are usually electroplated over the base metal.

Bind. The act of stitching or sewing the pages of a book or pamphlet together and enclosing them in a cover.

Blanket. A rubber-coated fabric which is clamped to the blanket cylinder of a lithographic press to transfer the image from the plate to the paper.

Bleed. That part of the printed image that extends beyond the trim edge of the sheet.

Blowup. An enlargement of art or photo.

Blueprint. See **Brownline.**

Bold-face type. Type that has wider strokes than normal, resulting in a blacker appearance on the printed page.

Booklet. A small book, usually with no cover or a soft cover.

Brochure. Any small pamphlet, booklet, or folded piece.

Brownline or **Brownprint.** A photoprint made from negatives or positives to serve as a final proof. Also called **Blueprint.**

Bulk. The thickness of a sheet of paper.

Camera. A light-tight box, usually consisting of a front and rear element joined together by a bellows. The front element supports the lens and the rear element, the film holder.

Chase. A rectangular metal frame in which a printing plate or type is locked. Used in letterpress process.

Chuck. An attachment for holding a workpiece in a machine, as in a press that prints onto glass containers.

Coated paper. Paper whose surface is coated with a mixture of clay and a glue made of casein, to make a smooth surface.

Cold type. In composition, any method of producing type proofs not involving hot, molten metal.

Collate. The assembling of sheets of paper or signatures into a given order.

Color sketch. A rough layout in color showing the approximate size, position, and color of all elements in a printing job.

Composition. The process of typesetting. The arrangement of lines and paragraphs in a piece of copy.

Contact print. A photographic print made by direct contact with a negative or positive under a light source on sensitized paper.

Continuous tone. A photographic image composed of infinite gradations of black and white. An image not screened.

Copy. Subject matter, whether words or art, in the preparation phase of printing.

Cover paper. Paper, usually of heavy basis weight, used for covers of books and magazines. Also called **Cover stock.**

Crop. The act of cutting off excess margins of photographs or artwork. Also cutting off unwanted portions.

Cut. In letterpress printing, a plate, usually mounted.

Densitometer. An electronic instrument for measuring the density or brilliance of ink images.

Dot. One of a series or pattern of discrete shadows formed by passing an image through a photographic screen.

Dot etching. Correcting or altering by hand the tonal values of halftones by changing the size of the halftone dots chemically.

Dummy. A miniature booklet prepared in advance to show the arrangement of pages, printed elements, color, and other features of a magazine, catalog, or other printed piece.

Duotone. Two-color printing of a black-and-white photo.

Electrotype. A high-fidelity duplicate plate made from an original plate or a type form.

Face. A particular style of type.

Farming out. A trade practice in which part of a printing job may be assigned to another printer or trade shop.

Flat. The assembled elements in the form of film, fastened to an opaque goldenrod sheet, which will be brought into contact with a sensitized printing plate.

Flexography. Rotary letterpress printing employing flexible rubber or plastic plates and fluid, fast-drying inks.

Flush left; flush right. Body type set to even margins left or right, respectively.

Folio. Page number.

Font. A complete assortment of characters and numbers in a particular style of type.

Form. Type and plates assembled in a chase according to the layout, ready for printing or for platemaking.

Fountain. Reservoir of ink or water in a press.

Gathering. The assembling of folded signatures in proper sequence.

Grain. The direction most paper fibers lie.

Gravure. Printing process employing intaglio or incised plates.

Grippers. Metal mechanical fingers or suction cups that grip the leading edge of a sheet as it passes through the press.

Grommet. An eyelet of metal or cardboard used to reinforce the hole in a paper tag.

Halftone. An image of a continuous tone photograph that has been passed through a screen. It is composed of a series of discrete shadows in a regular pattern. The size of the individual dots (and the absence of dots) represent the depth of the color, or the highlights, in the original photo.

Hard copy. Words or graphics produced on paper rather than simply displayed on a computer screen.

Imposition. The process of assembling pages so that they will be in proper sequence when the sheet is printed and folded.

Impression. A single pass of the press as it deposits an image on the sheet. In web offset printing, a single revolution of the impression cylinder.

Insert. A specially printed sheet or number of sheets bound into a publication.

Intaglio printing. Printing process employing plates with incised images. See **Gravure.**

Jog. The act of aligning to one uniform position the edges of a pile of paper.

Key plate. The plate used as a guide for registering all the other plates in a multicolor printing job.

Layout. Sketch or drawing, in color or black-and-white, of a proposed printing piece.

Lens. An arrangement of specially ground glass components glued together to form a complete optical unit of a given focal length.

Letterpress. Printing process employing plates cast or engraved in relief to form a printing surface upon which ink is deposited.

Line copy. Art or type for reproduction without a photographic screen.

Linotype. The trade name of a machine which automatically casts type in a one-piece line of metal from reusable matrices.

Lithography. The process employing a thin, flexible plate that repels or accepts ink and water. Also called **photo offset printing.**

Makeready. The technique of preparing a press so that the impression will be even and uniform across the entire printed surface.

Mechanical. Original art for a page or spread with all type and art elements fastened in place, ready for the camera.

Moire. (pronounced "more ray") Understandable pattern in a multicolor halftone caused by incorrect placement of one screen against another.

Montage. A grouping of photos or art to form a single unit.

Negative. In photography, a film on which the image has been fixed chemically so that dark areas are light and vice versa. Also, the relation of right to left is reversed.

Offset. A ghost image of a previous printing impression left on a sheet due to insufficient drying time between passes through the press. Also, an abbreviated term for offset printing.

Offset lithography. See **Lithography.**

Overlay. A transparent sheet of paper or film over a mechanical, usually used to indicate color separation.

Perfecting press. Any printing press that prints both sides of a sheet or web of paper on one pass through, or one revolution of the impression cylinder.

Photoengraving. The mechanical and chemical process of etching plates for relief printing, as distinguished from photolithography and photogravure.

Photogravure. The printing processes employing an intaglio plate.

Platen. A flat metal plate that holds paper to be printed.

Positive. In photography, a film on which the image has been transferred from a negative so that it matches the original in both light and dark areas and as to right and left.

Process printing. Usually associated with four-color printing, any printing process employing more than one plate to produce shades and tones of color.

Progressive proofs. A series of proofs designed to show the relationships of the four colors in process printing. A set of progressive proofs is normally arranged in the same sequence that will be followed on the press.

Proofreader. Person who compares the original copy with the typeset proof, making corrections on the proof as required. In many plants, proofreaders work in pairs, one holding the original copy and the other the proof.

Ram. The plunger of a hydrostatic press.

Ream. Five hundred sheets of paper of the same size and weight.

Register. The fit of two or more images on the same plate, flat, mechanical, or sheet.

Relief printing. See **Letterpress printing.**

Reproduction proof. A quality proof of a type form intended for photographic reproduction. If intended only for checking, it's called a **Proof.**

Reverse plate. A plate in which the background is black and the type matter white.

Saddle stitch (or Saddle wire). Process for binding booklets by means of a wire staple driven through the folded and punched edge of the booklet as it rests on the saddle of the stitching machine.

Screen printing. Printing process employing a fabric screen on which an image has been formed. Ink that is spread on the fabric by a squeegee is stopped from passing through to the sheet in nonprinting areas.

Set-off. See **Offset.**

Sewing. Process for binding booklets by sewing them together at the binding edge.

Signature. A large printed sheet after it has been folded.

Skid. A low, wooden platform upon which stacks or rolls of paper are placed. A forklift can slide under the skid to move the load.

Spiral binding. A method of binding a booklet by passing a spiral of wire through holes punched in the binding edge.

Stitch. See **Saddle stitch.**

Transparency. Normally a full-color positive intended for viewing with transmitted rather than reflected light.

Trim. To cut the edges of a book or magazine to final size.

Vacuum frame. A holder for transferring the image on a negative or positive to the photosensitive coating of a lithographic plate. The pressure inside the frame is reduced greatly to bring the film into perfect contact with the plate.

Vandyke print. A print made on sensitized paper used by offset lithographers as a proof of the flat. Also **Brownline.**

Web. A roll of paper fed through a web or rotary press.

With the grain. In folding, a fold parallel to the direction of the paper grain.